T0277024

SLAVERY

FROM AFRICA TO THE AMERICAS

SLAVERY

FROM AFRICA TO THE AMERICAS

Christine Hatt

CHERRYTREE
BOOKS

Cherrytree Books
50 Godfrey Avenue
Twickenham
TW2 7PF
UK

CHERRYTREE BOOKS

All rights reserved. No part of this publication may be reproduced, stored in a retrieval system, or transmitted, in any form, or by any means, electronic, mechanical, photocopying, or otherwise, without the prior permission of Cherrytree Books.

© **Copyright this edition Cherrytree Books 2020**

First Published by Evans Brothers

The Author asserts their moral rights. That the right to be identified as the Authors of this work has been asserted in accordance with the Copyright, Designs, and Patents Act 1988.

Every attempt has been made by the Publisher to secure appropriate permissions for material reproduced in this book. If there has been any oversight we will be happy to rectify the situation and written submissions should be made to the Publishers.

British Library Cataloguing in Publication Data (CIP) exists for this title.

ISBN   9781842349533
Title   Documenting History: Slavery from Africa to America

Printed in Malta by Melita Press

Acknowledgements

For permission to reproduce copyright pictorial material, the author and publishers gratefully acknowledge the following:
Cover: (poster) Peter Newark's American Pictures, (top right) The Goldsmiths Library of Economic Literature, University of London Library, (middle) Corbis-Bettmann, (bottom left) Peter Newark's American Pictures, (bottom right) Board of Trustees of the National Museums and Galleries on Merseyside/Walker Art Gallery, Liverpool
Title page: Courtesy of the Library of Congress
page 6 British Library/Bridgeman Art Library **page 7** (left) Archive Photos, (right) Corbis-Bettmann **page 9** (top) Museum für Volkerkunde, Berlin/Bridgeman Art Library, (bottom) Mary Evans Picture Library **page 10** Mary Evans Picture Library **page 11** Hulton Deutsch Collection Ltd **page 12** Mary Evans Picture Library **page 13** British Museum, London/Bridgeman Art Library **page 14** Peter Newark's Historical Pictures **page 15** British Library, London/Bridgeman Art Library **page 17** Library of Congress/Corbis **page 18** Pictorial Times/Mary Evans Picture Library **page 19** (top) Peter Newark's American Pictures, (bottom) Corbis-Bettmann **page 20** Private Collection/Bridgeman Art Library **page 21** Board of Trustees of the National Museums and Galleries on Merseyside/Walker Art Gallery, Liverpool **page 23** Peter Newark's American Pictures **page 24** Musée de la Cooperation Franco-Americaine/Bridgeman Art Library **page 25** Archive Photos **page 26** Wilberforce House, Hull City Museums, Art Gallery and Archives **page 27** Peter Newark's American Pictures **page 28** Hulton Deutsch Collection Ltd **page 29** Library of Congress/Corbis **page 30** Board of Trustees of the National Museums and Galleries on Merseyside/Merseyside Maritime Museum, Liverpool **page 31** Corbis-Bettmann **page 32** Peter Newark's American Pictures **page 33** Corbis-Bettmann **page 34** Peter Newark's American Pictures **page 35** (left) City of Bristol Museum and Art Gallery/Bridgeman Art Library, (right) Corbis-Bettmann **page 36** Peter Newark's Western Americana **page 37** Archive Photos **page 38** (top) Archive Photos, (bottom) Courtesy of the Library of Congress **page 39** Peter Newark's Western Americana **page 40** Hulton Deutsch Collection Ltd **page 41** Peter Newark's American Pictures **page 42** Peter Newark's American Pictures **page 43** Archive Photos **page 44** The Mansell Collection **page 45** Mary Evans Picture Library **page 46** Board of Trustees of the National Museums and Galleries on Merseyside/ Walker Art Gallery, Liverpool **page 47** Mary Evans Picture Library **page 48** (top) Wilberforce House, Hull City Museums, Art Gallery and Archives, (bottom) Mary Evans Picture Library **page 49** Hulton Deutsch Collection Ltd **page 50** Royal Commonwealth Society **page 51** The Mansell Collection **page 53** Peter Newark's American Pictures **page 55** Corbis-Bettmann **page 56** Peter Newark's American Pictures **page 57** (top) Corbis-Bettmann, (bottom) Peter Newark's American Pictures **page 58** Corbis Bettmann **page 59** Hulton Getty Picture Collection Limited

For permission to reproduce copyright material for the documents, the author and publishers gratefully acknowledge the following:
pages 6, 15, 17, 19, 39 (bottom) *Equiano's Travels* edited by Paul Edwards; Heinemann Educational Books. Reproduced by permission **pages 7, 25** From *The Secret Diary of William Byrd of Westover 1709-1712* edited by Louis B. Wright and Marion Tinling; The Dietz Press, 1941 **pages 7, 49** From *The History of Mary Prince, A West Indian Slave, Related by Herself* edited by Moira Ferguson. Ann Arbor: The University of Michigan Press, 1993. Reproduced by permission **pages 7, 55** From *The Negro in Virginia*; Hastings House **pages 9, 13, 21, 23, 27, 29 (bottom), 31, 33, 41, 45, 47** The Goldsmiths Library of Economic Literature, University of London Library **page 11** From *The Complete Works of Captain John Smith, 1580-1631* edited by Philip L. Barbour. Copyright © 1988 by the University of North Carolina Press. Used by permission of the publisher **pages 29 (top), 43** *Incidents in the Life of a Slave Girl* by Harriet Brent Jacobs; AMS Press **page 37** *Journal of a Residence on a Georgian Plantation in 1838-1839* by Frances Anne Kemble, edited by John A. Scott ©Random House, Inc. Reproduced by permission. **page 53** From *Narrative of the Life of Frederick Douglass, An American Slave*, Penguin USA. Reproduced by permission **page 57** From *A People's History of the United States* by Howard Zinn, reprinted by permission of Addison Wesley Longman Ltd **page 59** Reprinted by arrangement with the Heirs to the Estate of Martin Luther King, Jr., c/o Writers House, Inc. as agent for the proprietor, copyright 1963 by Martin Luther King, Jr., renewed 1991 by Coretta Scott King. While every effort has been made to secure permission to use copyright material, Evans Brothers apologise for any errors or omissions in the above list and would be grateful for notification of any corrections to be included in subsequent editions.

The author would like to thank the staff at the University of London Library for their help in researching this book.

❧Contents☙

LOOKING AT DOCUMENTS

This book charts the history of slavery in the Americas. It looks at the slave trade – the capture of people in West Africa, their transportation across the Atlantic and sale in the Americas. It considers how slaves lived, particularly in North America and the Caribbean islands. It highlights the enslaved people's constant fight against their enslavement. Finally, it examines the developments in Europe and the USA that brought slavery to an end.

To bring this story to life, *Slavery: from Africa to the Americas* uses a wide range of documents. These include accounts written by slaves themselves, extracts from the diaries of plantation owners, political and legal documents, speeches given by abolitionists (people who worked to abolish the slave trade, and later slavery itself), and many others. To make the documents easier to read, we have printed them in modern type. However, you will find photographs of some of the original documents alongside several of the extracts. Where there are difficult or old-fashioned words and phrases, these are explained in the captions around the documents.

When you are looking at the documents it is important to think carefully about their origins. When were they written – during a period when slavery was generally accepted, or when many people were beginning to question it? Where were they written – in a country where slavery was widespread, or from a distance? And, above all, who wrote them – are the authors doing their best to be truthful, or seeking to further their own aims? These questions and others like them will help you to work out how reliable a document is likely to be. But remember that no single document can give you a complete picture of the situation. Everyone has their own point of view. And people caught up in a situation can rarely see it as clearly as those looking back many years later.

A QUESTION OF LANGUAGE

Most of the documents in this book have been reproduced in their original form, keeping words and phrases in use at the time they were written. Some of the words that refer to black people are no longer used today, and are considered to be offensive. They have been kept in to give a true picture of life during the time of slavery, and to highlight the opinions held by some people at that time.

On these pages are a few extracts from the documents used in this book. They have been selected to give you an idea of the great variety of documents included, and to explain how and why some of the documents were written.

The autobiographies of ex-slaves often describe the harsh realities of their former lives in vivid detail. Extracts from Olaudah Equiano's fascinating story, first published in 1789, appear throughout this book.

One day, when all our people were gone out to their works as usual and only I and my dear sister were left to mind the house, two men and a woman got over our walls, and in a moment seized us both, and without giving us time to cry out or make resistance they stopped our mouths and ran off with us into the nearest wood.

Olaudah Equiano or GUSTAVUS VASSA

William Byrd

Like numerous wealthy American slave-owners, William Byrd of Virginia kept a journal (see page 25). It provides a revealing picture of plantation life.

I rose at 6 o'clock and read two chapters in Hebrew and some Greek in Lucian. I said my prayers and ate boiled milk for breakfast. I **danced my dance** and then went to the brick house to see my people pile the planks and found them all idle for which I threatened them soundly but did not whip them...

What does this mean? Some words and phrases in the documents are difficult to understand. The captions alongside the documents give explanations of the highlighted areas of text. You can find out what William Byrd meant by 'danced my dance' on page 25!

Political and legal documents, such as this handwritten first draft of the US Declaration of Independence, help to explain the historical background during the time of slavery (see page 35).

White abolitionists in the 19th century often rewrote slaves' memoirs. They wanted to make sure that the style of language would be acceptable to white readers. Mary Prince's autobiography was edited by her employer, Thomas Pringle (see page 49).

All slaves want to be free – to be free is very sweet... I have been a slave myself – I know what slaves feel... The man that says slaves be quite happy about slavery – that they don't want to be free – that man is either ignorant or a lying person...

Unlike Mary Prince's autobiography, the memories of American ex-slaves collected for the Federal Writers' Project in the 1930s were written down exactly as spoken. This example comes from Susie Melton (see page 55).

I was a young gal, about ten years old, and we done heard that Lincoln gonna turn the niggers free. Ol' missus say there wasn't nothin' to it. Then a Yankee soldier told someone in Williamsburg that Lincoln done signed the 'mancipation.

CHAPTER 1

ORIGINS

WEST AFRICA

West Africa was part of a major trading network long before the arrival of Europeans. From ancient times there were trade routes across the Sahara linking the North and West of the continent. Camel caravans took salt, copper, horses and other goods south to West Africa, and brought gold, ivory, kola nuts, hides, grain and slaves back to the North. After the rise of powerful Muslim states in North Africa in the early 8th century AD, the Islamic religion moved gradually south with the traders and trade goods.

Large cities developed along the Saharan trade routes (see map). Flourishing trade also led to the growth of great empires in the region. Just as elsewhere in the world empires rose and fell, but by the 15th century, when Europeans first arrived in West Africa, the wealthy empires of Songhai and Benin (see box) dominated the area.

Luxury goods such as gold and ivory had been imported from Africa into Europe by Arab traders for many centuries. But in the 1430s, as European shipbuilding and navigational skills improved, Portuguese sailors began to explore the West African coast for themselves.

TRADE ROUTES IN WEST AFRICA

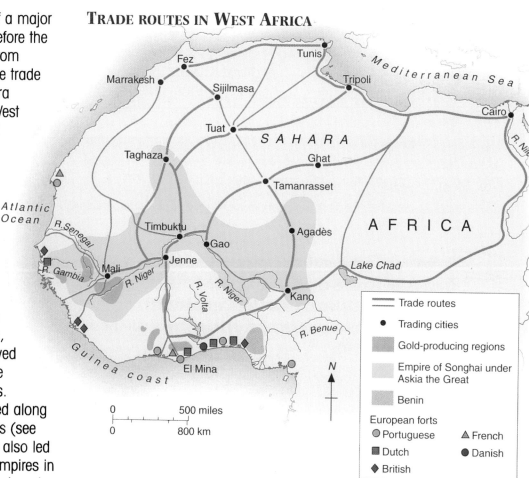

Ancient trade routes across the Sahara remained important for hundreds of years, but by the 17th century an increasing number of goods and slaves were transported out of the continent from European ports on the Atlantic coast.

By the 1460s the Portuguese had reached the Guinea coast (see map), and in 1481 they set up a trading post called El Mina (in modern-day Ghana).

The Portuguese were soon followed by adventurers from many other European nations, including the Netherlands, France and England. At first, these men raided African coastal communities and stole valuable goods. Then, gradually, they established more regular trading relationships. However, developments on the other side of the world were to alter this situation for ever. European exploration in the Americas (see pages 10-11) led to a great demand for slaves to work in the new colonies. Europeans did not want to do such work themselves, so they began to ship captured Africans across the Atlantic Ocean.

WEST AFRICAN EMPIRES

The Songhai Empire grew up around the city of Gao in the 14th century AD. It expanded rapidly under the Muslim ruler Askia Muhammad (known as Askia the Great) from the late 15th century, and remained powerful until it was invaded by Moroccans in 1591. The empire of Benin lay further south, in the rainforest regions along the coast. It was founded in the 11th century. Like the empire of Songhai, its success was based on commerce – the trade with Western Sudan for copper and other goods. By the 15th century, Benin was a major trading empire.

Artists from Benin made many brass sculptures of their *obas* (rulers) and other royal family members.

One of the great cities of Songhai was Timbuktu. This description of it was written in 1525 by a Moroccan traveller, Hassan ibn Muhammad, known in the West as Leo Africanus.

The city of Timbuktu in the 17th century. Most of its buildings were made of clay and straw, although wealthy people sometimes used bricks to construct their houses.

Artificers are skilled craftspeople.

Timbuktu was a bustling trading centre, providing a meeting place for North and West African **merchants**.

Salt was highly valued in West Africa, as it could be used to preserve and flavour food. It was one of the main imports from the north.

Camels were imported to Africa from Asia about 2000 years ago. Previously, horses had been used for transport.

Timbuktu was a centre of Islamic learning.

Barbary (the modern spelling) is the region of North Africa stretching from Morocco to the western border of Egypt.

...Here are many shops of **artificers**, and **merchants**, and especially of such as weave linnen and cotton cloth...Corne, cattle, milke, and butter this region yeeldeth in great abundance: but **salt** is very scarce heere; for it is brought hither by land from Tegaza, which is five hundred miles distant...The rich king of Tombuto [Timbuktu] hath many plates and scepters of gold, some whereof weigh 1300 poundes: and he keepes a magnificent and well furnished court. When he travelleth any whither he rideth upon a **camell**, which is lead by some of his noblemen; and so he doth likewise when hee goeth to warfare, and all his souldiers ride upon horses . **Here are great store of doctors, judges, priests and other learned men...**And hither are brought divers manuscripts or written bookes out of **Barbarie**, which are sold for more money than any other merchandize.

THE AMERICAS

Like Africa, the Americas were transformed by the arrival of Europeans in the 15th century. At that time the Caribbean was inhabited by three peoples, the Arawaks, the Caribs and the Tainos, while Central and South America were dominated by two great empires, the Aztec Empire in the Valley of Mexico, and the Inca Empire, based in Peru. North America was home to many Native American peoples, each with its own culture.

It was Christopher Columbus who commanded the first European fleet to reach the Caribbean. On 3 August 1492, Columbus sailed from Spain, hoping to find a new trade route to the riches of the East by travelling westwards. He had no idea that the Americas lay in between, so when he landed on a small island on 12 October, he thought that he had sailed right around the world and reached Asia. Columbus claimed the lands that he 'discovered' for Spain. Spanish adventurers soon arrived in the Caribbean. They forced the local people to work for them in mines and plantations. Many thousands of Native Americans died as a result of brutal treatment, or from unknown European diseases, such as smallpox, to which they had no immunity.

In 1519, the Spanish *conquistador* (conqueror) Hernán Cortés invaded the mainland of Central America. He destroyed the Aztec capital of Tenochtitlán and brought the whole civilisation to an end.

The Inca empire was conquered by another Spaniard, Francisco Pizarro, in the 1530s, and about ten years later, the region of modern-day Brazil was invaded and settled by the Portuguese.

A similar story unfolded in North America. The Spanish took Florida in 1565, while the French

THE AMERICAS

By the early 17th century, Europeans had settled many areas of North and South America.

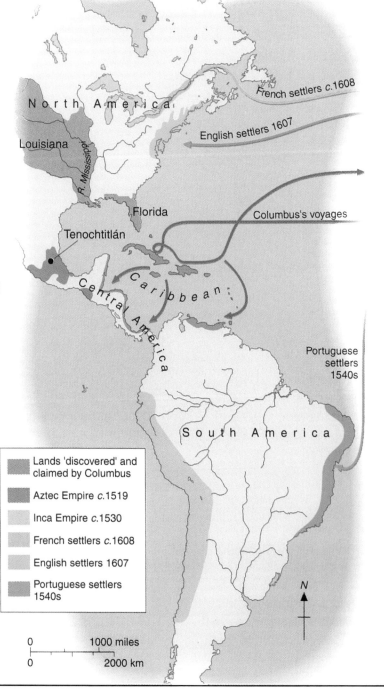

The fight for Tenochtitlán

Legend:
- Lands 'discovered' and claimed by Columbus
- Aztec Empire c.1519
- Inca Empire c.1530
- French settlers c.1608
- English settlers 1607
- Portuguese settlers 1540s

Map labels: North America, Louisiana, R. Mississippi, Florida, Tenochtitlán, Central America, Caribbean, South America, French settlers c.1608, English settlers 1607, Columbus's voyages, Portuguese settlers 1540s

Scale:
0 — 1000 miles
0 — 2000 km

settled part of Canada and in 1682 claimed a vast region to the west of the River Mississippi, which they called Louisiana. The first English colony on the mainland was established in Jamestown, Virginia, in 1607. By 1732, there were 13 English colonies along the east coast. To survive, the English colonists had to work the land.

Some Native Americans worked as field labourers, but more common was the use of indentured servants, poor Europeans who received free passage to America in return for years of unpaid work. The first Africans were brought to North America in 1619, and from about 1680 the use of black labourers increased dramatically.

The early English colonies in North America were established along the east coast, where many Native American peoples lived. Powhatan was the chief of one of these peoples. This extract comes from a speech made by him to some English settlers in 1609. Powhatan is replying to rumours that the settlers are about to begin a war to force the Powhatan people off their land.

English settlers land on the banks of the Potomac River in Virginia in 1634, while Native Americans look on.

The Native Americans knew the territory of the east coast extremely well – much better than the English colonists. For this reason they were often able to avoid capture.

In the early years of colonisation, the Native Americans traded maize and other crops with the English.

Copper and **hatchets** (small axes) were some of the goods the English traded with the Powhatan in return for food.

Large numbers of the early English colonists starved to death. Many others owed their survival to the Powhatan, who provided them with Indian corn (maize) and other foods.

What will it availe you to take that by force you may quickly have by love, or to destroy **them that provide you food?** What can you get by warre, when we can hide our provisions and **fly to the woods?** whereby you must famish by wronging us your friends....Thinke you I am so simple, not to know it is better to eate good meate, lye well, and sleepe quietly with my women and children, laugh and be merry with you, have **copper, hatchets,** or what I want being your friend: then be forced to flie from all, to lie cold in the woods, feed upon Acornes, roots and such trash, and be so hunted by you, that I can neither rest, eate nor sleepe...Let this therefore assure you of our loves, and every yeare our friendly trade shall **furnish you with Corne**; and now also, if you would come in friendly manner to see us, and not thus with your guns and swords as to invade your foes.

AGRICULTURE AND TRADE

European interest in the Americas flourished because there was money to be made from the products of the new colonies.

One of the main sources of profit for the Spanish was the gold and silver of the South American mainland. From the 1520s, the Spaniards shipped these precious metals from their new colonies back to Spain. They seized the gold and silver artefacts of the conquered Aztec and Inca empires (see pages 10-11), and they forced the local people to work in the gold and silver mines. Between 1500 and 1650, the Spanish sent more than 200 tonnes of gold and 16,000 tonnes of silver back to their homeland.

The Spanish also quickly discovered that sugar cane would grow well in the tropical climate of the Caribbean islands. Sugar cane had been grown in Portugal, Spain and other Mediterranean countries from the 8th century AD. In 1493, Columbus took the first sugar cane plants to the Caribbean. At first, the Spanish settlers forced local Native Americans to work in the new sugar cane plantations. But so many Native Americans

Native Americans smoked tobacco as a medicine and during religious ceremonies. The European word 'tobacco' probably comes from the Arawak word *tobago*, which meant 'a roll of tobacco leaves used for smoking'.

died from ill-treatment that there was soon a severe labour shortage. As a result, sugar cane was harvested by some of the first enslaved Africans to be transported to the Caribbean. Sugar cane was also transplanted to the South American mainland, when the Portuguese set up the first sugar plantations in Brazil in the 1540s.

In the 17th century, other European nations began to claim land in the Caribbean. The English occupied Barbados in 1625 and Jamaica in 1655, while the French took over Martinique and Guadeloupe in 1635, and St Domingue, western Hispaniola, in 1697. The sugar plantations established in these new colonies were all worked by enslaved Africans.

In the English settlements of North America (see page 11), Virginian farmers grew rich from the proceeds of tobacco-growing, as generations of Europeans became addicted to this so-called 'stinking weed'. Other important exports were rice, grain, timber, tar and a blue plant dye called indigo.

A SPOONFUL OF SUGAR

The increasing availability of sugar in Europe turned it into a common cooking ingredient. It was also used to sweeten the new drinks that were arriving from the colonies – coffee and chocolate (in the form of cocoa beans) from South America, tea from China and later India. In 1650, about 30,000 tonnes of sugar were shipped from the Americas to Europe. By 1850, the figure had gone up to 900,000 tonnes. Demand for rum, molasses and other products made from sugar also soared.

When new fruits and vegetables are introduced in shops today, supermarkets often provide leaflets explaining how to prepare and eat them. Similar instructions were used by people in the 17th and 18th centuries who wanted to smoke tobacco or drink coffee for the first time. They also wanted to know if these new products were good for them or might do them harm. This extract comes from *A Treatise on Tobacco, Tea, Coffee and Chocolate* which was first published in English in 1746. Here the author, Simon Pauli, deals with tobacco.

[Facsimile of pages 18-19 of the original treatise is shown, with the text:]

18 *A TREATISE on* for People of all Denominations to spend the whole of the Day smoaking Tobacco in Ale-Houses and Taverns? Nay, so fond are young and old Men of Tobacco, that the Father forgets the Interests of the Son, and the Son those of the Father for its Sake. Thus some Men use large Quantities of Tobacco, whilst, perhaps, their Families are starving at Home: Whereas what their industrious Parents had, with Toil and Care, amassed for their Use. Nay, such is the Madness of some Europeans, that they will, for a Trifle, dispose of their Goods, in order to gratify themselves with Tobacco.

King *James* the Sixth of *England* tells us, " that, among the *Americans*, a Servant ad- " dicted to the Smoaking of Tobacco, can " hardly find a Purchaser; so odious is that " Custom to the Authors of it themselves." We *Europeans*, however, are so infatuated and hood-winked, as yearly to sail to *America*, spare no Expences, and expose ourselves not only to Storms and Tempests, but also to Sickness and Death, for the Sake of Tobacco; and it is certain, that our Men, on their Return from *America*, spread through all *Europe* the Neapolitan Disease, which, as *Fio-rovanta* thinks, was endemial to the *Ameri-cans*, on Account of their eating human Flesh.

TOBACCO. 19 Flesh. This, to use the Phrase of *Agrippa*, *de Vanitat. Scientiarum*, Cap. 84. *is to pur-chase Death at a great Price.* The *Indians* and *Barbarians* have such an Averfion to the Abuse of Tobacco, that they severely chastise the *Ethiopians* and Slaves for it, and burn their Tobacco; probably, because they suspect that it renders them valetudinary, and disa-bles them to work; in which Situation they are a Burthen upon their Masters. Accord-ing to *Viganenus*, in *Lib. de Ritibus Mori-busq; Turcarum*; and *Johannes Chrysostomus Magnenus*, in *Exercitat. de Tabac. Exercit.* 6. §. 10. *Amureth*, the 4th Emperor of the *Turks*, by an Edict, prohibited the Use of Tobacco, under Pain of Death, left, by the Abuse of it, his Subjects should become ef-feminate, feeble, and barren. According to *Adamus Olearius*, in *Lib.* 3. *Cap.* 6. the Em-peror of *Muscovy*, in 1634, by an Edict pro-hibited the Importation of Tobacco and Snuff into his Territories, under the Penalty of being beat with Rods, and having the No-strils slit in Case of Disobedience: And the same Author says, he saw some who had these Marks of Infamy inflicted upon them. In *Lib.* 5. *Cap.* 31. he also tells us, that *Schach Abas*, the *Persian* Monarch, prohibited all Use of Tobacco in that Army, which he rais-ed against *Tameran Chan* under the Penalty of the Offender's having his Nose and Lips " cut C 2

Denominations can mean religious groups such as Baptists or Anglicans, but here the word simply means 'types'.

Those Authors, who have called Tobacco 'Herba rixosa', the Strife-producing Herb, and 'Herba insana', the Plant which excites Madness, seem not to have been very much in the wrong; for what is more frequent than for People of all **Denominations** to spend the whole of the Day smoaking Tobacco in **Ale-Houses and Taverns?** Nay, so fond are young and old Men of Tobacco, that the Father forgets the Interests of the Son, and the Son those of the Father for its Sake. Thus some Men use large Quantities of Tobacco, whilst, perhaps, their Families are starving at Home: Whereas some Children spend upon Tobacco what their industrious Parents had, with Toil and Care, amassed for their Use. Nay, such is the Madness of some Europeans, that they will, for a Trifle, dispose of their Goods, in order to gratify themselves with Tobacco.

Other popular venues for tobacco-smoking were the coffee houses that became widespread in London and other major European cities during the 18th century.

An 18th-century London coffee house. Rich gentlemen refresh themselves with strong coffee and tobacco smoked in long-stemmed pipes.

CHAPTER 2

THE TRIANGULAR TRADE

SLAVING

In many African societies, temporary enslavement as a household or farm labourer was a common punishment for crime or debt. These slaves were usually treated well and kept certain rights, for example the right to marry or own property. Africans had also provided slaves for the Muslim world for hundreds of years by selling prisoners-of-war into slavery.

The pattern of African slavery changed beyond recognition from the 15th century onwards. The first European adventurers kidnapped slaves by raiding villages along the coast. Naturally, such raids made Africans very unwilling to trade with the Europeans. So, gradually, a more organised business was established. Europeans bartered guns, alcohol and metal goods for criminals and prisoners-of-war with the African chiefs and kings. Soon, some rulers devised new 'crimes' for which the punishment was slavery, and others organised kidnapping raids far inland.

After one of these raids, the march from the interior to the coast was the second stage of a terrible nightmare for captured Africans. Bound in iron neck rings and linked together with chains, the prisoners staggered towards an unknown destination. On reaching the coast, they were imprisoned in the Europeans' forts and castles. As the trade grew, holding pens called barracoons were built, where Africans awaited the arrival of the slaving ships. European traders did not buy all the people who were brought from the interior. They preferred healthy men and women up to the age of 25, and they rejected the injured, the old, the weak and the sick.

According to the most accurate estimates of modern historians, at least 24 million Africans were captured to satisfy the European demand for slaves. Millions of them died from hunger and disease even before they reached the coast, but millions more had to endure the terrible sea crossing to the Americas.

Newly captured African slaves are forced to march to the Atlantic coast in this early 19th-century scene. Their necks are held in chains and shackles to prevent escape.

THE EFFECTS OF THE SLAVE TRADE

The European slave trade had a devastating effect on West Africa. The population declined and traditional ways of life broke down as Europeans encouraged African states to turn against one another, so that there would be more prisoners-of-war to sell as slaves. However, African rulers who were successful slave traders were able to found powerful new states. Two of the most important were Dahomey and Ashanti, which grew up on the Gulf of Guinea during the 18th century.

Olaudah Equiano grew up in an area of West Africa that is now part of Nigeria. In 1755, at the age of about ten, he was kidnapped by slave raiders. This account of his capture was published in his book *The Interesting Narrative of Olaudah Equiano or Gustavus Vassa the African* in 1789.

One day, when all our people were gone out to their works as usual and only I and my dear sister were left to mind the house, two men and a woman got over our walls, and in a moment seized us both, and without giving us time to cry out or make resistance they stopped our mouths and ran off with us into the nearest wood. Here they tied our hands and continued to carry us as far as they could till night came on, when we reached a small house where the robbers halted for refreshment and spent the night. We were then unbound but were unable to take any food, and being quite overpowered by fatigue and grief, our only relief was some sleep, which allayed our misfortune for a short time.

The title page of Olaudah Equiano's book shows the author in the dress of an 18th-century gentleman.

Equiano was soon separated from his sister, then sold four times from one group of slavers to another. For months he travelled in river canoes and on foot, until he finally reached the sea. To find out what happened to him next, turn to page 17.

CROSSING THE ATLANTIC

The slave trade between Africa and the Americas is often called the triangular trade, because most slaving voyages were made up of three separate stages. The first was the Outward Passage, in which goods such as guns, alcohol and iron bars were taken by ship from European ports to the coast of West Africa. The second was the Middle Passage, in which enslaved Africans exchanged for European goods were shipped across the Atlantic Ocean to the Americas. The third was the Inward Passage, the journey back to Europe with cargoes of sugar, rum, tobacco and other produce bought with the proceeds of slave sales.

The Middle Passage was an almost unbearable ordeal for the African prisoners. Men were crammed below decks with handcuffs on their wrists and leg irons around their ankles. On many ships, there were special platforms fitted between decks to accommodate an extra layer of slaves. Each layer was less than one metre high, making it impossible to stand upright. Women and children were kept in separate crowded quarters. They were usually unchained, but otherwise treated with as much brutality as the men.

The Atlantic crossing normally lasted about seven weeks, but could take longer in bad weather. Twice a day in good weather, slaves were taken up on deck for a short period of exercise. Below decks, living conditions for the prisoners grew worse and worse as the voyage progressed.

Many suffered from seasickness as well as much more serious illnesses such as dysentery and smallpox. Often they had no option but to vomit or relieve themselves where they lay, so that the holds became filthy and foul-smelling. These physical hardships were accompanied by terrible mental distress. Many Africans were so overcome with fear and despair that they threw themselves overboard. If rescued, they were cruelly beaten for trying to escape.

It is impossible to know exactly how many Africans met their deaths during the Middle Passage. However, the best estimates suggest that of the 13 million Africans who boarded ships in West Africa, only about 11 million reached the Americas alive.

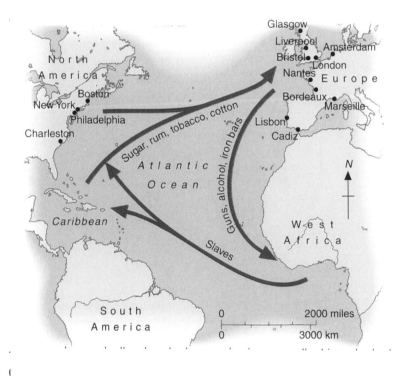

SHIPBOARD REBELLIONS
Africans did not sail off to their unknown fate without a struggle. Many successful rebellions took place on board slave ships. While they were on deck for exercise, enslaved Africans communicated with one another as best they could, and sometimes managed to overpower unwary sailors. Female slaves, too, played an important part in planning revolts. As they were allowed to move around the ships more than the men, they could often relay messages or even pass on weapons without attracting the attention of the crew.

THE *AMISTAD* REBELLION

One of the most famous shipboard rebellions took place in 1839 on the *Amistad*, a Spanish ship transferring about 50 slaves between ports on the Caribbean island of Cuba. The slaves had only recently arrived from Africa and their plan was to take over the ship and sail it back to their homeland. Led by Joseph Cinque, they armed themselves with huge knives designed for cutting sugar cane, killed the ship's captain and cook, and took control of the vessel. During the voyage to Africa, the *Amistad* was captured by an American ship. The slaves were first taken to the USA, but were later freed and allowed to make their way home.

Rebellion on board the *Amistad*

 Olaudah Equiano's book (see page 15) contains an account of his experiences in the hold of a slave ship. Here he tells of his feelings on first being forced below decks.

I was soon put down under the decks, and there I received such a **salutation in my nostrils** as I had never experienced in my life: so that with the loathsomeness of the stench and crying together, I became so sick and low that I was not able to eat, nor had I the least desire to taste anything. I now wished for the last friend, death, to relieve me; but soon, to my grief, two of the white men offered me eatables, and on **my refusing to eat**, one of them held me fast by the hands and laid me across I think the **windlass**, and tied my feet while the other flogged me severely.

This is Equiano's way of saying there was a terrible smell.

Many slaves refused to eat, through sheer misery or as a deliberate attempt to starve themselves to death. They were usually punished by flogging and forced to eat, because thin, weak slaves were worth little to their owners.

A **windlass** is a huge drum round which anchor chains are wound.

SLAVES FOR SALE

Traders paid little attention to the health and well-being of their slaves during the Middle Passage. Many enslaved Africans were ill, weak and totally wretched by the time they reached the Americas. But sickly looking slaves did not make money. So, as the ships approached the shore, slaves were frantically washed and shaved to make them more presentable and therefore more valuable. Traders even dyed the grey hair of older men to make them seem youthful.

There were two main kinds of slave sales, the auction and the scramble. In an auction, slaves were forced to parade one by one in front of buyers, or stand on a raised platform so that they could be clearly seen. A professional auctioneer sold each slave to the highest bidder.

Scrambles, on the other hand, were nothing less than free-for-alls. They were held either on board ship or in an enclosed area on land. At a pre-arranged time, would-be slave owners were allowed to rush into the midst of the huddle of slaves and simply grab those they wished to buy.

Before they were sold, enslaved Africans were first subjected to degrading body-searches. People treated them like animals, pulling back their lips to look at their teeth, peering into their eyes, prodding them in the back and stomach and even examining their sexual organs. Further misery and indignity awaited the slaves once the sales were over. Many were separated from relatives or

shipboard friends who had been sold to different owners. Some were branded with their owner's mark, and most were forced to take on new English names.

Many of the newly imported slaves died within a few years of reaching their destination. In the Caribbean islands and Brazil, where many slaves were employed in the exhausting work of sugar cultivation (see page 12), the number of slave deaths was higher than the number of children born to slaves. As a result, these colonies remained dependent on continued supplies of captured and enslaved people from West Africa.

SLAVE NAMES
As most slave owners were Christians, they often called their slaves after Biblical characters such as Abraham. Others preferred the names of famous people and gods from ancient Greece and Rome. However, some African-born slaves managed to keep their own names. One common boy's name was Sambo. Its original meaning was 'second son', although it was later used by white people as a patronising term for any black boy. Common girl's names were Sukey and Tillah.

African slaves were often branded with the mark of their 'owner'. This degrading treatment made it clear that many whites regarded slaves as just another possession, like their cattle.

Olaudah Equiano's slave ship took him to the island of Barbados, where he was sold in a scramble. This is his account of that event.

Slave auctions were advertised in newspapers and on posters. This poster is giving advance notice of a sale in Charlestown, in the state of Massachusetts.

We were not many days in the merchant's custody before we were sold after their usual manner, which is this: On a signal given (as the beat of a drum) the buyers rush at once into the yard where the slaves are confined, and make choice of that parcel they like best. The noise and clamour with which this is attended and the eagerness visible in the countenances of the buyers serve not a little to increase the apprehensions of the terrified Africans... In this manner, without scruple, are relations and friends separated, most of them never to see each other again. I remember in the vessel in which I was brought over, in the men's apartment there were several brothers who, in the sale, were sold in different lots; and it was very moving on this occasion to see and hear their cries at parting.

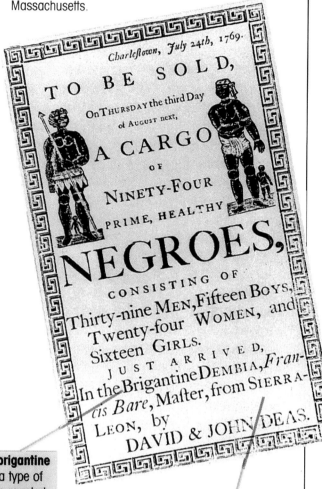

A **brigantine** is a type of two-masted sailing ship.

Sierra Leon, more commonly spelt Sierra Leone, was a region of West Africa.

An auctioneer calls for bids in a slave sale held in the city of Charleston, Virginia, in 1861.

GROWTH AND PROFIT

From small beginnings in the 15th century, the slave trade grew into a huge and successful business. It transformed the lives not only of enslaved Africans and colonial slave-owners, but also of merchants and workers in the European countries that began this ugly trade in humanity.

By the end of the 17th century, British slave traders had transported more slaves between Africa and the Americas than any other European country – a total of about 100,000 Africans. All British slaving ships operated under the control of the Royal African Company. However, demand for slaves in the British colonies was growing faster than supply, and plantation owners began to complain to the British government. So, in 1698, private individuals were permitted to enter the slave trade for the first time.

The number of slaving voyages soared. Between 1698 and the abolition of the British slave trade in 1807 (see page 47), about three million Africans were carried in British ships. Britain's major slaving ports, London, Bristol and Liverpool, flourished as never before. By 1780, Liverpool was the busiest transatlantic slaving port in Europe. The only check on its growth was the inability of builders to construct ships fast enough.

The city of Amsterdam, in the Netherlands, in the 16th century.

As the slaving business grew so, too, did trade in European goods shipped out to Africa, and in tropical produce brought back from the Americas. Workers who manufactured trade goods such as copper, glass, textiles and guns, were in constant employment. Ship-builders, outfitters and repairers were always in demand, as were sailors. Importers who processed and distributed sugar, tobacco and cocoa beans flourished.

There was more. Transatlantic voyages were always risky, so merchants took out insurance, fuelling a rapid growth in this financial service. And someone had to look after all the money that merchants were making, so the banking industry boomed too. Governments were not left out of this bonanza either. They charged duties and taxes on produce shipped to and from the colonies, then sat back as money flooded into their treasuries.

SLAVING NATIONS

Britain was by no means alone in its commitment to the slave trade. At various times, the cities of Bordeaux and Marseille in France, Cadiz in Spain, Lisbon in Portugal and Amsterdam in the Netherlands (pictured here) were all slaving ports. North American colonists also sailed to Africa to capture slaves for themselves. The first North American slaving ship, the *Desire*, left Massachusetts in 1637. However, the majority of slaves for North American owners were provided by the British until after the American Revolution (see pages 34-5).

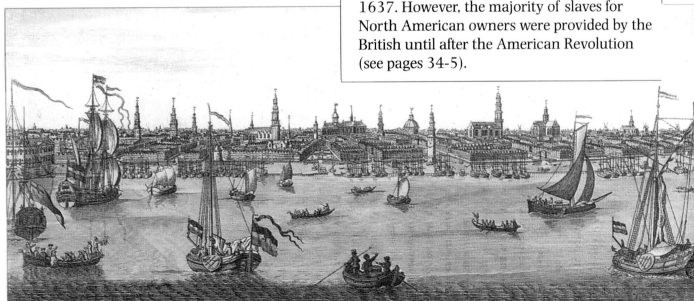

A Liverpool slave ship in about 1780.

During the 18th century, Liverpool was transformed by the trade with Africa. A man called James Wallace made a written record of the port as it grew wealthy from the profits of slavery. This extract from Wallace's book, *A General and Descriptive History of the Ancient and Present State of the Town of Liverpool* (1795), highlights the feverish atmosphere of business activity and greed.

A **bandbox** is a small box, usually used for storing hats. The author is explaining that people in Liverpool are so eager for profit that they will trade even something as small as a hat box for African slaves.

It was not only merchants and shipowners who took part in the slave trade. Lawyers, grocers, barbers and many others bought small shares in slaving ships and received some of the profits in return.

This great annual return of wealth, may be said to pervade the whole town, increasing the fortunes of the principal adventurers, and contributing to the support of the majority of the inhabitants; almost every man in Liverpool is a merchant, and he who cannot send a **bale**, will send a **bandbox**, it will therefore create little astonishment, that the attractive African **meteor** has from time to time so dazzled their ideas, that almost every **order of people** is interested in a **Guinea** cargo...

A **bale** is a bundle of cloth or other material.

A **meteor** is a shooting star. This is a small object that shines brightly as it falls through the sky. The African trade dazzled the people of Liverpool with its success, just as a meteor dazzles with its brightness.

Guinea was the name used at this time to describe the coast of West Africa between Cape Verde and Angola.

CHAPTER 3

SLAVE LIFE

FARMS AND PLANTATIONS

The majority of the enslaved Africans brought to the Americas ended up working on farms and plantations. Slaves who were newly arrived from Africa had to be prepared for harsh field labour. At first farmers and planters (plantation-owners) gave them relatively easy work to do, such as weeding, gathering stones and looking after animals. This process was known as 'seasoning'.

In the American North (see map), most farms were small, employing an average of only three to four slaves per farm. Here it was not uncommon for white masters to till the ground alongside their slaves. In the tobacco- and wheat-growing states of the Upper South, most farms were not much larger than those in the North. But slaves made up a much greater proportion of the population than in the North, where many people lived in cities.

In the Deep South, vast rice plantations were cultivated by enslaved Africans. By 1720, there were so many black slaves in South Carolina that they outnumbered the white inhabitants two to one. The rice farmers operated a 'task system', in which slaves were given a job to complete each day. Only when their task was finished were they allowed to stop work. Masters rarely visited their fields, leaving slave-drivers to supervise the slaves' work.

In the sugar plantations of the Caribbean, slaves were in the majority almost everywhere, often outnumbering whites by at least ten to one. On these plantations, a punishing form of labour called the 'gang system' was used (see box). In the fields, women toiled alongside the men, doing the same back-breaking work. Slaves usually worked a six-day week, their only work-free day being Sunday.

North
Upper South
Deep South

Vermont
Maine
Minnesota
N.H.
Wisconsin
Mass.
Michigan
New York
R.I.
Pennsylvania
Conn.
Iowa
N.J.
Indiana   Ohio
Del.
Illinois
Md.
Virginia
D.C.
Missouri
Kentucky
North Carolina
Tennessee
Arkansas
South Carolina
Texas
Mississippi
Georgia
Atlantic Ocean
Alabama
N
Louisiana
Florida

N.H.	New Hampshire
Mass.	Massachusetts
R.I.	Rhode Island
Conn.	Connecticut
N.J.	New Jersey
Del.	Delaware
Md.	Maryland
D.C.	District of Columbia

0   800 miles
0   1200 km

THE GANG SYSTEM

Africans working in the sugar plantations of the Caribbean were put into gangs depending upon their age and their fitness for hard physical labour. Young, old and sick slaves carried out light work, such as weeding. The strongest slaves carried out the most demanding tasks, such as cane-cutting. Slave gangs were constantly watched by 'drivers' who used the whip readily. It was harsh, punishing work. The slaves worked from about five o'clock in the morning to six o'clock at night, with only a short break for breakfast, and a slightly longer one for lunch.

Sugar was the most important crop on many Caribbean islands. Managing a sugar plantation was a complicated task, so many experienced planters wrote books giving advice to new farmers. The month-by-month instructions below are a simplified version of *The Planter's Kalendar* written by Gordon Turnbull, a planter on the island of Grenada, in 1785.

Take off means cut down or harvest.

Bill is short for 'billhook', a huge knife with a curved blade used to cut sugar cane.

Stock means animals, such as mules.

Hole means to make holes in the ground in order to put the new plants in.

The **great gang** was sometimes also called the first gang, and the small gang the second gang. On the biggest plantations, three separate gangs were often used to work the land.

Masters often wrote about the care of their slaves. But they rarely put their words into practice.

JANUARY   Cut down the canes left standing over from the last crop; if their sugar quality is poor, improve it by mixing them with good old **rattoons**.

FEBRUARY   **Take off** the ripest plants, unless this month is too wet. In that case, weed the young plants and spread dung round those that require it.

MARCH   The ripe canes are now yellow, and seem to invite the **bill**. The **mill** should operate constantly, so that most canes may be cut this month.

APRIL   If the rest of the canes can be taken off in this dry month, it should be done, yet neither the slaves nor the **stock** should be over-worked.

MAY If the planter cut all his canes last month, he will now be able to **hole** some land for a spring plant, and give his young plants a thorough weeding.

JUNE   If land has been prepared for a spring plant, it should be put in before the end of this month. The young plants should have another weeding.

JULY The crop should now be over. Dung should be put on the fields which are to be first planted, and the trash should be collected into heaps.

AUGUST Dig out the stumps and begin holing the land with the **great gang**, that is the able people. The small gang should weed the young canes.

SEPTEMBER   Continue to hole with the great gang and to weed with the small gang. This is a wet month, so every negro should be provided with a jacket.

OCTOBER   Continue to hole with the great gang and to weed with the small gang. The land which was holed in August may be planted this month.

NOVEMBER   Plant the prepared land and weed all the young plants before the month's end. Do not make the slaves remain long in the field under heavy rains.

DECEMBER   The business of planting should be finished early this month. Serve the negroes with their yearly allowance of clothes at Christmas.

Rattoons are the roots of old sugar canes.

Cut canes were taken to the plantation **mill** where they were crushed to extract the sugar.

Slaves cutting sugar cane on a plantation in the American Deep South in about 1850. Slave 'drivers' watch, ready to punish slacking with the lash of a whip.

DOMESTIC SLAVERY

Although most slaves were field labourers, many worked either as domestic servants or as skilled craftspeople on the plantations and in the towns.

On plantations everywhere, female slaves worked as general domestic servants, cleaning, polishing and washing. Other women had more specialised roles such as dressmaker, cook or nurse. All were at the beck and call not only of their masters, but also of their masters' wives, who were often more harsh than their husbands. However, for many female slaves the worst aspect of slavery, both domestic and in the fields, was the difficulty of avoiding the sexual demands of their white masters.

Male slaves were able to take on a wider variety of jobs away from the fields than the women, and the bigger the plantation, the more options were open to them. Possible occupations included painter, carpenter, groom, blacksmith and shoemaker, and some slaves combined several of these roles. Men who had a skilled trade enjoyed more freedom than most other slaves. They could move around the plantation to carry out their tasks, and were sometimes allowed to leave it altogether. This happened mainly when masters hired them out to a neighbouring planter for a fee.

There was a difference between the North American colonies and the Caribbean islands in the domestic environment as well as in the fields (see page 22). Most North American planters lived on their plantations and regarded them as home. The richest planters lived in a Great House on a home estate while owning several other, smaller farms in the neighbourhood. In contrast, many wealthy Caribbean planters lived for much of the year in Europe, leaving their plantations in the care of overseers. Those who did remain often built Great Houses where they enjoyed all the luxuries that money could buy. However, there was little for planters to do on the islands, so many of them lapsed into a life of drunkenness, crude behaviour and sexual excess.

The Great House on Thomas Jefferson's estate of Monticello in Virginia. Thomas Jefferson was the third president of the USA. He kept slaves despite believing that slavery was wrong. He also owned six other slave-worked farms.

William Byrd

William Byrd was a Virginia planter who from 1709 to 1712 recorded the details of his daily life in a diary. This is known as his 'secret' diary because it was written in a type of shorthand. Modern scholars have decoded Byrd's shorthand to reveal a fascinating account of 18th-century plantation life. This extract dates from 27 February 1711, and gives a clear idea of how many domestic slaves were commonly treated.

Lucian was an ancient Greek writer of the 2nd century AD.

Byrd often writes this in his diary. His **dance** was a kind of physical exercise that he believed kept him fit and healthy.

Planters often called slaves their **people**.

Jenny was a domestic slave in Byrd's household.

I rose at 6 o'clock and read two chapters in Hebrew and some Greek in **Lucian**. I said my prayers and ate boiled milk for breakfast. **I danced my dance** and then went to the brick house to see **my people** pile the planks and found them all idle for which I threatened them soundly but did not whip them. The weather was cold and the wind at northeast. I wrote a letter to England. Then I read some English till 12 o'clock when Mr. Dunn and his wife came. I ate boiled beef for dinner. In the afternoon Mr. Dunn and I played at billiards. Then we took a long walk about the plantation and looked over all my business. In the evening my wife and little **Jenny** had a great quarrel in which my wife got the worst but at last by the help of the family Jenny was overcome and soundly whipped. At night I ate some bread and cheese. I said my prayers and had good health, good thoughts, and good humor, thank God Almighty.

A page from William Byrd's secret diary, written in his own special shorthand. The month and year of the entries are noted at the top of the page, while the exact day is listed in the margin.

IN THE TOWNS

One category of slaves who had more freedom than most were urban slaves. Planters who kept town houses required servants to look after them there as they did on the plantations. Town-based businessmen also liked to be waited on by domestic servants. However, town houses were often not large enough to provide accommodation for anyone other than the owner and his family. Slaves were therefore allowed to live in the slave quarters that grew up in most major towns.

SLAVE FAMILIES

Slaves' working lives were dominated by the demands of their owners. But during their free time, most did their best to establish family lives to help them endure the hardships of their everyday existence.

In North America, slaves normally had to ask the permission of their masters before marrying. Some slaves married partners from neighbouring estates, known as 'marrying abroad'. This was discouraged by planters, as it meant that male slaves spent what little free time they had visiting their wives and relatives. However, slaves could not leave their plantations without a pass, so remained under their masters' control.

As long as it was cheap and easy to import slaves from Africa, planters in the Caribbean discouraged slaves from marrying and having children. Young children were of no use to them on the plantations, and in any case huge numbers of slave children died within weeks of birth from disease and lack of food. However, in the late 18th century planters became worried that the supply of slaves from Africa was about to end, so they began to encourage men to marry on their home plantation and to father the next generation of slaves.

In North America and the British Caribbean slave marriages had no legal status and slave families were not officially recognised.

Nevertheless, slaves struggled against all the odds to preserve the family network. Most planters did not think twice about separating members of a slave family. Male slaves were often sold or hired to another estate, leaving wives to bring up their children alone.

Children inherited their mothers' status as slaves. Some slave children were put to work as early as four years of age, doing jobs such as picking up rubbish or pulling out weeds. Older children were expected to look after the younger children during the day, while mothers were at work in the fields. Between about ten and 14, children became full-time domestic slaves or field labourers. Many were sold to other plantations and never saw their mothers again.

A group of slaves dance and make music during their free time on the island of Dominica in the Caribbean. The chance for relaxation was rare in lives dominated by long days of hard physical labour.

FOOD AND FREEDOM

Many enslaved Africans had their own small gardens where they grew fruits and vegetables and kept a few goats or pigs. The slaves ate much of this food themselves, but often took any spare produce to local markets to sell or exchange for other goods. In this way, they could buy clothes and other wares that their masters would not provide.

The first slaves lived in farm outbuildings, or in dormitories. But as slave families became more numerous, many planters on large estates provided a tiny log cabin for each family to live in. The following account of a slave cabin in South Carolina comes from *The Life and Adventures of Charles Ball*. Published in 1836, this was the autobiography of a man who served as a slave in the American South for 40 years. You can read more of Ball's story on pages 31, 33 and 41.

Ball was newly arrived on this plantation. The overseer had just introduced him to a fellow-slave, whose cabin he was to share.

About a quarter of a mile from the dwelling house, were the huts, or cabins, of the plantation slaves, or field hands, standing in rows... These cabins were thirty-eight in number; generally about fifteen or sixteen feet square; built of hewn logs; covered with shingles, and provided with floors of pine boards... In these thirty-eight cabins, were lodged two hundred and fifty people, of all ages, sexes and sizes... I followed my **new friend** to his cabin, which I found to be the **habitation** of himself, his wife, and five children. The only furniture in this cabin consisted of a few blocks of wood, for seats; a short bench, made of a pine board, which served as a table; and a small bed in one corner, composed of a mat, made of common rushes, spread upon some corn husks, pulled and split into fine pieces, and kept together by a narrow slip of wood, confined to the floor by wooden pins.

Shingles are wooden tiles.

Habitation means 'home'

A row of identical slave cabins on the Hermitage Plantation in Savannah, Georgia.

SLAVE RELIGION

Slaves were sustained not only by their family lives, but also by their religious beliefs. The first enslaved Africans came from many different regions of West Africa with many different religions. However, these religions often had elements in common. Many taught that the world was inhabited by good and evil spirits, and that dead ancestors watched over the lives of their descendants. Ruling over both spirits and people was one High God. These beliefs travelled with the slaves to the Americas.

In some parts of the Caribbean, African beliefs developed into a religion known as obeah. Male and female obeah priests used their powers to contact the spirit world in order to influence events in the material world, for example curing a sick person, or causing sickness in an enemy. Many planters were terrified of obeah priests, fearing their ability to harm whites and to rouse slaves to rebellion. As a result, punishments for practising obeah were severe, often including the death penalty.

In the American colonies controlled by Catholic powers – the Portuguese, Spanish and French – African slaves were baptised as Christians from the earliest days of slavery. But in the British-controlled, Protestant Americas, planters showed little interest in converting their slaves. Many feared that to accept slaves as Christians was to acknowledge that black slaves were equal to their white masters – a dangerous message as far as the planters were concerned.

In North America, this attitude began to change when a Christian movement, called the Great Awakening, swept through the north-eastern colonies from the 1750s. This movement was based on the preaching of Baptist, Methodist and Presbyterian ministers. They emphasised that all people, black and white alike, were sinners, but that all could be saved by Christianity. Slaves heard a message of freedom and equality in this new style of preaching, and many converted. Baptist and other missionaries also spread the Christian message in the Caribbean. In the late 18th and early 19th century, blacks developed their own churches, where the singing, dancing and preaching were influenced by African forms of worship.

A white slave-owner, his family and his slaves listen intently to a sermon from a black preacher in South Carolina.

George Whitehead (1714-70) was an English Methodist who spent many years in America. His preaching helped to inspire the religious movement known as the Great Awakening (see page 28).

Most white ministers preached to slaves about the need for obedience, but said little about the equality of all people in the eyes of the Lord.

Harriet Jacobs was a former American slave who published her autobiography, *Incidents in the Life of a Slave Girl*, in 1861. This shortened account of a white Anglican clergyman's attempts to preach to a group of slaves is taken from it. You can read more from Harriet Jacobs on page 43.

When the Rev. Mr. Pike came, there were some twenty persons present. His text was, 'Servants, be **obedient** to them that are your masters according to the flesh, with fear and trembling, in singleness of your heart, as unto Christ.' Pious Mr. Pike brushed up his hair till it stood upright, and, in deep, solemn tones, began: 'Hearken, ye servants! Give strict heed unto my words. You are rebellious sinners. Instead of serving your masters faithfully, which is pleasing in the sight of your heavenly Master, you are idle, and shirk your work. God sees you.'

This is part of an Act passed in 1789 for the regulation of slaves in the British Caribbean island of Jamaica. It shows what strict measures the island authorities used to try to stamp out the practice of obeah.

... any Slave who shall pretend to any supernatural power, and be detected in making Use of any Blood, Feathers, Parrots Beaks, Dog's Teeth, Alligator's Teeth, broken Bottles, Grave Dirt, Rum, Egg Shells, Cotton Tree Juice, or any other Materials relating to the Practice of Obeah or Witchcraft, in order to affect the Health or Lives of others, or promote the Purposes of Rebellion, shall... suffer Death, or be confined to hard Labour for Life.

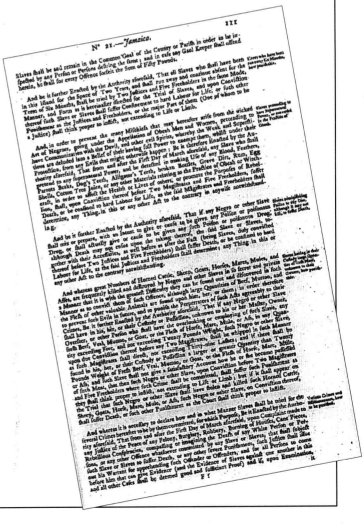

SLAVE LAWS AND PUNISHMENTS

Masters tried to control their slaves by introducing rules and laws that governed almost every aspect of their lives. With these laws came harsh punishments for breaking them.

There were large numbers of black people in North America by the middle of the 17th century. Some had managed to buy their freedom with money or labour (see pages 38-9), but most were slaves. Each colony had its own laws, but everywhere the main rules were the same. Black slaves were the 'property' of their owners, and had to do whatever their owners required of them. They received no pay, were not allowed to own

property, to give evidence against white people, or to marry legally. Slaves were forbidden to leave their plantations without permission from their masters.

Similar laws applied in the British Caribbean, where slaves had absolutely no rights. These laws were drawn up by the colonial authorities on each island, which were controlled by the planters. On most islands, slaves were also forbidden to become Christians or even to learn to read and write.

Different laws for the control of slaves were introduced in other parts of the Caribbean. In 1685, the *Code Noir* (Black

Code) was drawn up in France for use throughout the French islands. The Spanish islands were also centrally controlled, with a code known as *Las Siete Partidas*. Both these codes were severe, but gave slaves more rights than British laws, for example the right to marry. But, in practice, French and Spanish slave owners generally did as they pleased.

Punishments for law-breaking were harsh. Slaves were whipped for the smallest offence, sometimes an ear or a hand was cut off, and in the worst cases, slaves were buried

'Pass Jane about town for one month till 10 o'clock at night.' Slaves were allowed to go out only if their owners gave them written permission. This slave pass, dating from 1845, was found by chance in a book bought in Savannah, Georgia, in about 1935.

A pair of shackles dating from the 18th century. Metal 'leg irons' like this were fitted around slaves' ankles to prevent them from moving.

alive or hanged. In the British Caribbean, execution by hanging or burning was favoured for those slaves who took part in rebellions.

From the late 18th century, the anti-slavery movement in Britain forced the government to attempt to control the excessive violence of some planters. As a result, limits on slave punishments were introduced in many colonies. In 1807, when Britain passed a law making the trade in slaves illegal (see pages 46-7), new slave codes were introduced to control the treatment of slaves still further – at least in theory. But, until slavery itself finally came to an end, many planters continued to punish their slaves mercilessly.

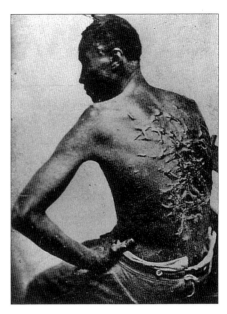

Whipping often resulted in terrible, permanent scars. This photograph of 1863 shows a man who was savagely whipped by his master on a cotton plantation in Louisiana.

These accounts of slave punishments used in the American South appear in the autobiography of Charles Ball (see page 27). The first deals with whipping. The second explains 'the punishment of the pump', in which slaves were forced to stand naked under a powerful jet of water.

Cat-gut is tough cord made from dried animals' intestines.

Buckskin is the skin of a male deer or a sheep.

Tanning is the process by which animal skin is turned into leather.

The whip used by the overseers on the cotton plantations is different from all other whips that I have ever seen. The staff is about twenty or twenty-two inches in length, with a large and heavy head, which is often loaded with a quarter, or half a pound of lead, wrapped in **cat-gut**, and securely fastened on, so that nothing but the greatest violence can separate it from the staff. The lash is ten feet long, made of small strips of **buckskin, tanned** so as to be dry and hard, and plaited carefully and closely together.

When the water first strikes the head and arms, it is not at all painful; but in a very short time, it produces the sensation that is felt when heavy blows are inflicted with large rods, of the size of a man's finger. This perception becomes more and more painful until the skull bone and shoulder blades appear to be broken in pieces. Finally, all the faculties become oppressed; breathing becomes more and more difficult; until the eyesight becomes dim, and animation ceases. This punishment is in fact a temporary murder.

RUNAWAYS

The conditions of slavery were so harsh that some enslaved Africans ran away, intending never to return. Others regularly left their home plantations for short periods without permission, to visit members of their family or to escape from the constant demands of their masters.

Young, single males with no family ties were the most frequent runaways. Most fled alone or in pairs, as large groups were easier for slave owners to find. Slaves who did not plan to be away long stayed with relatives or hid in woods or farm buildings until they felt ready to return. When they did go back, slaves were often punished severely. Sometimes, planters used dogs to hunt for runaways. Savage dogs proved very successful at catching – and sometimes killing – runaway slaves.

After the American Revolution (see pages 34-5), states in the North of the USA began to abolish slavery. As a result, thousands of slaves from the South tried to make their way north – as many as 1000 per year by the middle of the 19th century. These intrepid blacks used a wide variety of methods to escape. Many stowed away on boats heading for northern ports. Others walked by night and hid in forests and swamps by day until they reached the border. The American government passed two laws in an attempt to stop this flood of runaways. The Fugitive Slave Law of 1793 made it illegal to shelter runaways, while a law passed in 1850 made it legal for Southern slave-owners to hunt escaped slaves and take them back from the North.

Some runaways formed Maroon communities. The word 'Maroon' comes from the Spanish *cimarron*, which means 'dwelling on mountain-tops' and was first used to describe runaways who settled in the mountains of the Spanish-'owned' island of Hispaniola in the early 16th century. Large Maroon communities of runaways later grew up in Brazil and Surinam on the South American mainland, and on Caribbean islands such as Dominica and, in particular, Jamaica. In North America, there were Maroons in the Great Dismal Swamp on the border between Virginia and North Carolina. Maroons survived both by growing crops for themselves and by raiding plantations for food and for weapons.

Dogs, particularly bloodhounds, were often used to track down runaways in the swamps and fields of the American South.

Charles Ball (see page 27) came from the North but was taken to the South to work as a slave on the cotton plantations. He made his first escape in 1810, and rejoined his wife and children in Virginia. Following the death of his wife six years later, Ball remarried and had four more children. However, in 1830 he was recaptured and taken back to the cotton plantation. Escaping once more, Ball returned northwards to find that his second wife and children had also been sold to the South. He never saw them again. This account from his autobiography tells part of the story of his first escape.

I was awake before day, and as soon as there was light enough to enable me to see my way, I walked on, until about eight o'clock, when I came to a river, which I knew must be the Appalachie. By sounding the river with a pole, I found the stream too deep to be waded, and I therefore prepared to swim it. I kept a straight line from the place of my entrance to the opposite side, and when I had reached it, stepped on the margin of the land and turned round. Within twenty feet of me, in the very line that I had pursued in crossing the river, a large alligator was moving in full pursuit of me, with his nose just above the surface. The alligator can swim twice as fast as a man, and had I been ten seconds longer in the river, I should have been dragged to the bottom, and never again been heard of.

THE UNDERGROUND RAILROAD

The Underground Railroad was the name given to a network of land and sea routes leading from the slave states of the American South to the free states of the North, and to Canada beyond. Vast numbers of slaves travelled along these routes from the late 18th to the mid-19th century. Many did not travel alone, but were escorted by 'conductors' who knew where to find food and shelter along the way. These brave men and women risked their lives to help others escape. The most famous of the conductors was former slave Harriet Tubman, who had herself fled from the South. She acted as conductor on more than 19 journeys from Maryland to the North with more than 300 runaways. She told them: 'You'll be free or die.'

Harriet Tubman (left) stands alongside just two of the many slaves she helped to escape.

CHAPTER 4

REVOLUTION AND REBELLION

THE AMERICAN REVOLUTION

The 13 colonies of British North America were ruled from London, despite the fact that they were not represented in parliament. This was a cause of growing resentment, which eventually spilled over into the American War of Independence.

The move towards independence began after the Seven Years' War between France and Britain (1756-63). Victory gave the British control over vast areas of North America previously claimed by the French. However, the war also left the British with huge debts. The British parliament decided to pay off some of the debts by imposing new taxes on the colonists. These measures caused widespread anger and riots.

The first shots of the War of Independence were fired in Lexington, Massachusetts in April 1775. On 2 July 1776, representatives from 12 of the colonies voted unanimously for America to break away from British control. Thomas Jefferson, a planter from Virginia, drafted the Declaration of Independence. It stated that all people were created equal and had a right to liberty.

The war caused turmoil as it raged across North America for seven years (after 1781 the fighting

One of the many taxes Britain imposed on its American colonies was an import duty on tea. Colonists, many in Native American dress, boarded tea ships in Boston harbour on 16 December 1773 in protest. Then they simply dumped the cargo overboard. This event became known as the Boston Tea Party.

was mainly at sea). Many slave-owners left their plantations to join the Patriot (American) army. Others fled with their slaves to colonies away from the conflict, such as Kentucky and Tennessee. In the absence of their masters, thousands of slaves took the opportunity to run away.

The war came to an end in September 1783, when Britain officially acknowledged the independence of the United States of America. Americans now had to establish a new system of government. They did this by drawing up a set of laws, called the constitution, which came into force in 1789. But despite statements in the Declaration of Independence about the liberty and equality of all people, the new constitution did not abolish slavery. In fact, it stated that the slave trade (not slavery itself) would be stopped no earlier than 1808.

 This extract is taken from the Declaration of Independence, which was drafted by Thomas Jefferson in 1776.

Thomas Jefferson

Unalienable rights means rights that cannot be taken away.

A copy of Thomas Jefferson's original, handwritten version of the Declaration of Independence.

SLAVES IN THE WAR

Many slaves fought in the war. Thousands of slaves joined the British troops, particularly after the British governor of Virginia, Lord Dunmore, offered freedom to any slave prepared to join him in the fight against the American rebels. Large numbers of slaves were killed in the fighting, while still more died from smallpox and other diseases. At the end of the war in 1783, the British sold some of the survivors back into slavery. Others were freed and taken either to Britain or to the British colony of Nova Scotia in eastern Canada. Some slaves also served in the Patriot army, often in return for their freedom. But most slaves did not wish to fight on the side of the people whom they saw as their persecutors.

We hold these truths to be self-evident: That all men are created equal; that they are endowed by their Creator with certain **unalienable rights**; that among these are life, liberty, and the pursuit of happiness...

NORTH AND SOUTH

The twin ideals of liberty and equality that inspired the American Revolution also led many people in the USA to fight for the abolition of slavery. A wide variety of groups took up the abolitionist cause. Black activists argued their case forcefully in writing and in speeches. White politicians set up anti-slavery organisations. Christian groups such as the Quakers and the Baptists opposed slavery on religious grounds. All this activity brought results. By 1827, every state in the North had abolished slavery. In some states, all slaves were freed immediately. In others, no existing slaves were freed, but their children were given the right to freedom once they reached a certain age.

Abolitionist arguments in the North were based on the principle that slavery was wrong. However, slavery was also less important in the North than it was in the South. Many people in the North lived in towns and growing numbers had industrial jobs. As a result, there was no need for armies of slaves to work on plantations. In addition, there were many white immigrants in the region eager to take on the work formerly done by slaves.

In the states of the Deep South (see map page 22), the situation was very different. Slave numbers actually increased during the years following independence. This was a result of the need for slaves to work in the new cotton plantations (see pages 40-1). As it seemed likely that the slave

trade would be abolished in 1808 (see page 35), thousands of new slaves were imported directly from Africa to beat the deadline. Even following abolition, the trade in slaves continued illegally, but after 1808 most slaves were bought from owners in the North and the Upper South (see box) who no longer needed them. At the same time, state assemblies in the South made it more difficult for slaves to gain their freedom. By the early 19th century, slavery was on the increase in the rural states of the Deep South, but in decline in the urban states of the North.

Field slaves on a farm in 19th-century South Carolina. Some till the ground while others sort the crop of sweet potatoes.

Frances Kemble was an English actress. In 1834 she married an American, Pierce Butler, and settled with him in Philadelphia. Pierce inherited a huge, slave-worked rice and cotton plantation in Georgia, and made a short visit with his wife. From January to April 1839, Frances kept a journal recording her stay in Georgia, and pouring out her horror at the events she witnessed. In 1863 her *Journal of a Residence on a Georgian Plantation in 1838-1839* appeared in both England and the USA.

This extract from the journal highlights the misery caused by the practice of transferring slaves between states. This occurred most commonly between states of the Upper South and those of the Deep South. However, in this case a slave (Joe) is being moved from one state of the Deep South to another state further west.

Frances Kemble hoped that her journal would persuade both English and American readers that the anti-slavery cause was just.

Mr Butler was Frances' husband.

TOBACCO CRISIS

In the states of the Upper South, such as Virginia and Maryland, many whites actively opposed slavery in the years immediately following independence. But, just as in the North, the planters' actions were not influenced by high moral principles alone. In the late 18th century there was a crisis in the tobacco industry. Over-production had exhausted the soil and caused prices to fall, so many planters began to grow different crops such as wheat and corn. Others became livestock farmers. As a result, they needed fewer people to work the land and could free some slaves without causing a labour shortage. However, slavery remained important throughout the region. Slaves were essential not only for the work they did, but for the income produced by their sale to the Deep South.

Early the next morning, while I was still dressing, I was suddenly startled by hearing voices in loud tones in **Mr Butler's** dressing room, which adjoins my bedroom, and the noise increasing until there was an absolute cry of despair uttered by some man. I could restrain myself no longer, but opened the door of communication and saw Joe...raving almost in a state of frenzy, and in a voice broken with sobs and almost inarticulate with passion, reiterating his determination never to leave this plantation, never to go to Alabama, never to leave his old father and mother, his poor wife and children, and dashing his hat, which he was wringing like a cloth in his hands, upon the ground, he declared he would kill himself if he was compelled to follow **Mr King**.

Mr King was the Butlers' overseer. He had just resigned in order to set up his own plantation in Alabama, and Mr Butler had given Joe to him as a present.

FREE BLACKS

Not all black people in the Americas remained slaves until abolition. Many were freed by their owners. This was known as 'manumission'. As a result, large communities of free blacks grew up throughout the region.

Planters granted manumissions for a variety of reasons. Some slaves became too old or ill to work, and masters no longer wanted to pay for their food and shelter. Others were freed as a token of gratitude. Many planters freed the children they had fathered by slave women. Occasionally a planter freed all his slaves, for example if he had become a Christian and believed that his new faith did not permit slavery.

Some slaves were able to buy their own manumission. They saved money by using skills such as carpentry or dress-making, or selling surplus food grown in their gardens. But in many

Richard Allen was a minister in the Methodist church until experience of racial discrimination persuaded him to set up a church for blacks only. This was the African Methodist Episcopal Church, founded in 1816.

colonies, particularly those in the British Caribbean, planters made it very difficult for slaves to buy their freedom, often charging more than slaves could afford. For most slaves, this method of manumission remained out of reach.

By 1860 there were almost 500,000 free blacks in the USA, making up 11 per cent of the country's total black population. However, to be free was not to be equal. In much of the Caribbean, free blacks were allowed to take only the lowest-paid jobs, and were denied access to education. The same kinds of restrictions applied in much of the USA, including most of the Northern states, where free blacks were not allowed to vote or to join the armed forces. Segregation – the separation of blacks and whites – was commonplace, in towns, and in schools and churches.

The response of free blacks to this situation was to set up their own schools, churches and places of employment. Black churches, often Baptist or Methodist, flourished everywhere. One of the most influential was the African Methodist Episcopal Church, founded by Richard Allen in the USA in 1816. Many community organisations were also set up. These organisations frequently played a major part in the abolition movement (see page 52).

ISAAC and ROSA, Emancipated Slave Children, From the Free Schools of Louisiana,
Photographed by KIMBALL, 477 Broadway. N.Y.
Entered according to Act of Congress, in the year 1863 by GEO. H. HANKS, in the Clerk's Office of the U. S. for the Sou. Dist. of N.Y.

This photograph of two young children, Isaac White (aged eight) and Rosa Downs (aged six), was used as part of a fund-raising campaign for black schools.

Despite the deep prejudice against them, many free blacks managed to have successful careers. One man who triumphed against all the odds was John Mercer Langston (1829-97). Langston was the first black lawyer in the state of Ohio, and the first black Congressman from the state of Virginia. He later became US minister to Haiti. As well as carrying out his official duties, Langston worked tirelessly for black causes. This is part of a speech that he gave in 1869 to the First Black National Labor Convention, an organisation promoting the rights of black workers.

All over the South and among the colored people of the North, workmen in gold, silver, brass, iron, wood, brick, mortar, and the arts, are found doing skillfully and at usual wages the most difficult tasks... perhaps the most accomplished gunsmith among the Americans is a black man, an ex-slave of North Carolina... It is perhaps true, too, that the most finished cabinet-maker and blacksmith of our country is of the same class. And it is said to be the fact that the most valuable invention given us by the South, the cotton plough, was the **creature of a slave's genius...**

This means 'was invented by a slave'

Olaudah Equiano (see page 15) bought his own manumission. His last master, Robert King, agreed to free him for 40 pounds in the belief that his slave would never be able to obtain this amount. But Equiano gradually saved the money. King reluctantly agreed to let him go, and sent Equiano to register the manumission. Here Equiano takes up the story:

When I got to the office and acquainted the Register with my errand he congratulated me on the occasion and told me he would **draw up my manumission for half price**, which was a **guinea**. I thanked him for his kindness, and having received it and paid him I hastened to my master to get him to sign it, that I might be fully released. Accordingly, he signed the manumission that day, so that before night, I who had been a slave in the morning, trembling at the will of another, was become my own master and completely free. I thought this was the happiest day I had ever experienced;...

There was a charge for registering a manumission as well as for the document of manumission itself.

A **guinea** was a gold coin used in Britain until 1813 and worth 21 shillings (£1.05).

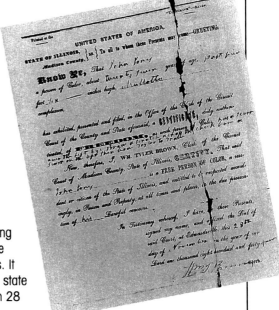

A certificate granting freedom to a slave called John Jones. It was signed in the state of Illinois, USA, on 28 November 1844.

KING COTTON

Until the late 18th century, most American cotton was grown in just four states – Virginia, North Carolina, South Carolina and Georgia. However, by the 1830s, cotton-growing had spread far to the west. And wherever there were cotton plantations, there were slaves.

There were two main reasons for the spread of the cotton plantations, the invention of the cotton gin (see box), and the increase in demand for raw cotton. By the late 18th century, the Industrial Revolution in Britain had produced a successful textile industry. New machines such as Richard Arkwright's spinning frame were able to spin cotton faster than ever before. Similar changes were taking place in other parts of Europe and the north-eastern USA. As a result, anyone who could provide raw cotton was sure to make money.

The growth in cotton production was staggering. In 1790, the USA produced a mere 3000 bales of cotton. By 1860, output was 4.8 million bales, three-quarters of the world's cotton crop. The overwhelming importance of cotton led one Southerner to proclaim that cotton was king, and the cotton-growing states became known as the 'cotton kingdom'.

As cotton-growing expanded, so did the number of slaves needed to work in the fields. Many were brought from other states by professional slave traders. Slaves dreaded being sold to states in the west. They sometimes called it being 'sold down the river', a reference to the River Mississippi which ran through many of the most important cotton-growing areas. Being sold down the river meant separation from family, friends and familiar places, usually for life.

Young children carry out the back-breaking work of cotton-picking on a Texas plantation in the late 19th century.

In this extract from his autobiography (see page 27), Charles Ball explains how a cotton gin works and the care needed to operate it.

Formerly there was no way of separating the cotton, from the seed, but by pulling it off with the fingers – a very tedious and troublesome process, – but some one from the North, at length, discovered the gin, which is a very simple, though very powerful machine. It is composed of a wooden cylinder, about six or eight feet in length; surrounded at very short intervals, with small circular saws... It is necessary to be very careful in working about a cotton-gin; more especially in removing the seeds from before the saws; for if they do but touch the hand, the injury is very great. I knew a black man, who had all the sinews of the inner part of his right hand, torn out... and the flesh of his palm cut into tatters, by carelessly putting his hand too near the saws, when they were in motion...

This American advertisement for sewing cotton dates from the same period as the plantation photograph (page 40). But it presents a much rosier, less realistic, picture of plantation life.

WHITNEY'S COTTON GIN

The type of cotton grown in 18th-century plantations was known as long-staple cotton. To thrive, it needed a warm, wet climate and good soil. Short-staple cotton, on the other hand, would grow anywhere reasonably warm. The disadvantage of short-staple cotton was that it was extremely difficult to separate the seeds from the fibre needed to make cloth. However, in 1793 a machine devised by American inventor Eli Whitney provided the answer. Called a cotton gin, it separated the seeds and the fibres of short-staple cotton quickly and efficiently. Within 40 years of the invention of the cotton gin, cultivation of short-staple cotton was widespread in Alabama, Mississippi and Louisiana. Ten years later, Arkansas and Texas had become major cotton-growing areas, too.

An early, hand-operated cotton gin. Larger, machine-operated versions were introduced during the 19th century.

REBELLION IN THE USA

The first slave revolt of any size in North America took place in September 1739. This uprising was started by about 20 enslaved Africans in Stono, South Carolina. The slaves marched towards Spanish-controlled Florida, where they hoped to be granted freedom. As they travelled, they recruited many other slaves, swelling their numbers to about 150. At the same time, the slaves killed several planters and destroyed houses and farms on their way. However, the rebellion was short-lived. White soldiers from the local army soon caught up with the slaves, shooting many on sight. More were executed later, once they had been questioned.

In Virginia in 1800, a slave called Gabriel Prosser attempted to organise a rebellion on a much larger scale, gathering together over 1000 slaves to march on the city of Richmond. However, an informer betrayed him and he was executed, together with more than 30 others.

The rebellion planned by Denmark Vesey, a free black, in 1822 was quashed even before it began. Vesey hoped to burn down the town of Charleston in South Carolina, then stir up all the slaves in the area to revolt. His preparations were careful and comprehensive. Thousands of slaves were forewarned of the uprising, and many secretly made weapons such as daggers and bayonets. However, the very fact that so many slaves knew about Vesey's plan made discovery likely. Once local whites heard about the conspiracy, Vesey and 35 others were hanged.

The mainland revolt that caused the white population the most serious concern was the rebellion led by Nat Turner. Turner was a domestic slave and preacher in Southampton County, Virginia. In August 1831, he saw an eclipse of the Sun which sparked off a religious vision. Believing this to be a sign from God that he should begin a revolt, Turner went on the rampage. During a period of just two days, he and about 70 other slaves killed at least 60 whites. Inevitably, however, the small slave band was eventually overcome by planters and soldiers armed with guns. Turner managed to evade capture for about two months, but was finally caught and hanged. About 55 other rebels were also executed.

After two months on the run, rebel-leader Nat Turner is finally cornered by one of his pursuers.

SLAVE UPRISINGS IN THE USA

N

Virginia
Richmond 1800
Southampton County 1831

South Carolina
Stono 1739
Charleston 1822

Atlantic Ocean

First Seminole War 1818
Second Seminole War 1835
Florida

0   400 miles
0   600 km

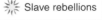
Slave rebellions

The Nat Turner rebellion terrified the white citizens of Virginia. In an attempt to ensure that nothing like it ever happened again, they took their revenge on the entire black population. About 200 black slaves were murdered by white mobs as a direct result of the rebellion. This account of the terrible aftermath of the revolt comes from Harriet Jacobs' autobiography (see page 29).

Powder here means 'gunpowder'.

Insurrection is another word for rebellion.

Shot is the collective name for metal pellets that can be fired from guns.

A **bucking paddle** was a wooden device shaped like a paddle, specially made to beat people.

Those who never witnessed such scenes can hardly believe what I know was inflicted at this time on innocent men, women, and children, against whom there was not the slightest ground for suspicion. Colored people and slaves who lived in remote parts of the town suffered in an especial manner. In some cases the searchers scattered **powder** and **shot** among their clothes, and then sent other parties to find them, and bring them forward as proof that they were plotting **insurrection**. Every where men, women, and children were whipped till the blood stood in puddles at their feet. Some received five hundred lashes; others were tied hands and feet, and tortured with a **bucking paddle**, which blisters the skin terribly.

Many fighters from both sides of the conflict died during the Battle of Okeechobee Swamp, in the Second Seminole War.

THE SEMINOLE WARS

Until 1819, the Florida region of the USA was controlled by the Spanish. This region was the home of the Native American Seminoles, and it had also become a place of refuge for runaway slaves. Seminoles and blacks lived in the same villages, and often intermarried. The American government was unhappy about this situation, and decided to take Florida from the Spanish.

In 1818, the Americans began the border raids of the First Seminole War, and a year later the Spanish handed over Florida. However, the Seminole and black inhabitants remained.

American settlers began to move to the region, and in 1834 the Seminoles were ordered to move out. They refused to go. In 1835 the Second Seminole War erupted, with blacks fighting alongside Seminoles against their common enemy. The bitter struggle continued until 1842, when most of the Seminoles surrendered and were forced to move west, to the area of modern-day Oklahoma. Their black co-fighters were allowed to go with them.

REBELLION IN THE CARIBBEAN

There were more slave rebellions in the Caribbean than in North America, particularly on the islands where black slaves hugely outnumbered whites. Rebels were punished severely, and many were executed, but this did not prevent unrest from breaking out regularly.

In Jamaica there were many disturbances, with frequent skirmishes between whites and Maroons (see page 32). In 1732, British soldiers captured three Maroon towns and sparked off the First Maroon War. Neither side was able to achieve complete victory so, in 1739, the British signed a peace treaty with the Maroon leader, Cudjoe. One of the conditions of this treaty required the Maroons to help the British to recapture runaway slaves and put down rebellions. In 1760, the Maroons honoured this agreement by capturing and killing the leader of a slave revolt, named Tacky. However, the treaty did not prevent the Maroons of one area from starting the Second Maroon War in 1795. Fighting continued for two years, ending with the deportation of many Maroons to Nova Scotia in Canada, then to Sierra Leone in West Africa.

The site of the only slave rebellion to overthrow white rule was not British Jamaica, but French St Domingue. In 1789, the French Revolution replaced the king of France with a government based on the principles of liberty, equality and fraternity. Slaves on St Domingue hoped the new government would set them free. In August 1791, the situation boiled over into rebellion. About 100,000 slaves marched across the island, killing, burning and looting. When the abolition of slavery was declared in an attempt to restore order, British and Spanish troops invaded, hoping to take over the island in the confusion. These troops were eventually defeated by a black army, led by an ex-slave called Toussaint l'Ouverture.

In 1796, Toussaint l'Ouverture became Governor-General of St Domingue, and by 1800 the island was under his control. But in 1799 a new ruler came to power in France – Napoleon Bonaparte. He wanted to reconquer St Domingue and bring back slavery. He sent an army to the island in 1801. Toussaint and his generals led a brilliant campaign against the French, forcing a compromise. However, the French went back on their word, captured Toussaint and took him to France, where he died in 1803. The French were eventually defeated and, in 1804, St Domingue was declared a republic and renamed Haiti, 'the land of the hills'.

British soldiers and Jamaican Maroons discuss peace terms following a period of fighting. Despite their best efforts, the British never managed to quash these fiercely independent people.

This extract is taken from an account of the St Domingue rebellion prepared by members of the General Assembly of the island. Their report was read to the National Assembly (the French parliament) in Paris on 3 November 1791 and gave a vivid impression of the chaos and terror caused by the revolt.

Sugar was the main product of St Domingue.

An **attorney** is a lawyer or other legal official.

A **refiner** works in a sugar factory where raw sugar is purified.

Expires means 'dies'

A **musket** is a long-barrelled gun that fires large metal balls.

A **cutlass** is a curved sword.

In the night, between the 22d and 23d, twelve negroes reach the **sugar-house** of Noé's plantation at Acul, seize upon the apprentice **refiner**, drag him before the great house, where he **expires** under his wounds. His cries, bring out the **attorney** of the estate, who is laid breathless on the ground by two **musket-balls**. The wretches proceed to the apartment of the head refiner, and assassinate him in his bed. A young man, lying sick in a neighbouring chamber, they leave for dead under the blows of their **cutlasses**; yet, he has the strength to crawl to the next plantation, where he relates the horrors he has witnessed.

When Toussaint l'Ouverture (left) was taken prisoner by Napoleon, he told the French leader: 'By overthrowing me, you have only cut down the trunk of the tree of liberty of St Domingue. Its roots will grow back, for they are many and deep.'

THE BAPTIST WAR

The largest slave rebellion in Jamaica, the Baptist War, took place in 1831. Sam Sharpe was a black Baptist deacon who was a powerful and persuasive preacher. He read in the newspapers about the campaign in Britain for the end of slavery (see pages 48-9), and he urged slaves to demand immediate payment of wages. He arranged for a strike to begin on 27 December 1831. Over 20,000 slaves took part, destroying plantations and killing 14 whites. It took the local army and British soldiers over two months to quell the revolt. Over 200 slaves, including Sam Sharpe, were executed. Many more were severely flogged.

ABOLITION AND AFTER

THE END OF THE SLAVE TRADE

In the late 18th century, the campaign in Britain to bring an end to the slave trade began to gain supporters. Many people opposed the trade in enslaved Africans on moral grounds, particularly members of religious groups such as the Quakers, Methodists and Baptists. In 1787, some of these campaigners established the Society for the Purpose of Effecting the Abolition of the Slave Trade (the Abolition Society). Many black people living in Britain also actively worked for abolition. These included Ottobah Cugoano, who wrote a book attacking slavery, and Olaudah Equiano, whose autobiography and lecture tours helped to promote the abolitionist cause.

At this time, the main concern of the abolitionists was to bring an end to the capture of slaves in Africa and their sale in the Americas. By ending the trade in slaves, abolitionists hoped to force slave-owners to treat their workers better. The campaigners argued that if planters could no longer expect regular supplies of new labour from Africa, they would have to give their slaves enough food, housing and medical care to keep them healthy and able to have children.

Some wealthy British families employed black slaves, as this 18th-century painting, *The Family of Sir William Young*, shows.

Those who defended the trade in enslaved Africans included British planters, ship-owners, merchants and bankers. They stated that slavery was essential to the economic well-being of Britain, as well as of the British Caribbean. Politicians from cities such as Liverpool (see pages 20-1) argued that bringing an end to the slave trade would cause financial ruin for many businesses.

In Parliament, the anti-slavery campaign was led by William Wilberforce. Following the creation of the Abolition Society, he worked closely with one of the Society's campaigners, Thomas Clarkson. Clarkson went to the ports of Bristol and Liverpool to collect evidence about the slave trade – particularly about conditions for the slaves on board the slave ships. He then passed this information to Wilberforce, so that it could be publicised in parliament. Wilberforce made numerous unsuccessful attempts to introduce a bill to outlaw the slave trade. Finally, in 1807, the Abolition Act was passed and the British slave trade was abolished.

John Wesley was an 18th-century British religious leader. He founded the Christian church known as the Methodist church. Wesley was appalled at the inhumanity of slavery, which he witnessed on a visit to Georgia with his brother Charles. In 1774, he published a book called *Thoughts upon Slavery*, in which he gave his answers to all the common arguments put forward to defend slavery. Below is his response to the idea that slavery is necessary for the economic good of a nation.

Leading figures in the struggle for abolition in Britain. Sharp and Macaulay campaigned against the slave trade in the courts, while Wilberforce, Clarkson and Buxton took the fight to parliament.

'But the furnishing us with Slaves is necessary, for the Trade, and Wealth, and Glory of our Nation:' Here are several mistakes. For 1. Wealth is not necessary to the Glory of any Nation; but Wisdom, Virtue, Justice, Mercy, Generosity, Public Spirit, Love of our Country. These are necessary to the real Glory of a Nation; but abundance of Wealth is not... It is far better to have no Wealth, than to gain wealth, at the expence of Virtue. Better is honest Poverty, than all the Riches bought by the tears, and sweat, and blood of our fellow-creatures.

HEROES OF THE SLAVE TRADE ABOLITION.

FREEDOM AND APPRENTICESHIP

The end of the British slave trade did not mean an end to slavery itself, nor did conditions for slaves improve as much as the abolitionists had hoped (see page 46). In the 1820s, the abolitionists started a new campaign – this time for the emancipation (freedom) of all slaves.

Campaigners continued to fight against slavery on moral grounds, but a new economic argument helped them too. British sugar was expensive because slave plantations were inefficient. Planters were only able to sell their sugar because the government imposed taxes on non-British sugar, making it even more expensive. This was contrary to the new idea of free trade, introduced by the Scottish economist Adam Smith. He argued that Britain's economy would be more successful if goods could be imported directly from the cheapest source, without having to pay taxes. Many industrialists, who wanted inexpensive raw materials for their factories, supported this view.

Following Wilberforce's retirement in 1825, Thomas Buxton became the leading anti-slavery campaigner in Parliament. He was helped in his work by the Reform Act of 1832, which for the first time allowed members of parliament to be elected from new industrial towns such as Birmingham and Manchester. These men wanted slavery to end so that free trade could be established.

Many coins and medals were made to promote and commemorate the abolition of slavery. This example dates from 1834.

In 1833, Buxton introduced the Emancipation Bill to abolish slavery in the British colonies. The bill was passed, but only slaves under six years of age were freed immediately. All older slaves had to serve an apprenticeship, a period of four to six years during which they were obliged to work for nothing for up to 45 hours per week. To oversee this change-over period, the British government appointed 150 Special Magistrates. However, it soon became clear that the apprenticeship scheme was not practical, so it was brought to an early end. At midnight on 31 July 1838, all British slaves were freed.

The treadmill was introduced in the British Caribbean during the final years of slavery. Slaves had to turn the mill with their feet while hanging from a bar. This was an exhausting and degrading punishment.

Many black people in Britain contributed to the anti-slavery campaign. One of these was Mary Prince. She arrived in London from Antigua in 1828 and found employment as a servant in the household of Thomas Pringle, the secretary of the Anti-Slavery Society. Pringle persuaded Mary to write a book about her experiences. *The History of Mary Prince, A West Indian Slave, related by herself* was published in 1831. It opened the eyes of many people to the horrors of slavery. This is an extract from it.

All slaves want to be free – to be free is very sweet... I have been a slave myself – I know what slaves feel... The man that says slaves be quite happy about slavery – that they don't want to be free – that man is either ignorant or a lying person. We don't mind hard work, if we had proper treatment, and proper wages like English servants, and proper time given in the week to keep us from breaking the Sabbath. But they won't give it; they will have work – work – work, night and day, sick or well, till we are quite **done up**; and we must not speak up nor look amiss, however much we be abused. And then when we are quite done up, who cares for us, more than for a lame horse? This is slavery.

Done up here means 'exhausted'.

Slaves in the British-controlled island of Barbados take to the streets in 1833 to celebrate emancipation.

ENFORCING ABOLITION

Britain was just one of many countries to abolish the slave trade in the early 19th century. In 1814, France followed suit, as did Spain in 1820. Newly independent Brazil brought its trade to an end in 1830. However, many ships continued to carry Africans between West Africa and the colonies because fines for breaking the law were low and profits were high.

Britain sent Royal Navy ships to the West African coast to stop this illegal activity. Between 1820 and 1870, the Navy stopped nearly 1600 slaving vessels in these waters and freed the people on board. Many of these men and women were taken to Sierra Leone in West Africa, a colony established by the British in 1787 for the settlement of freed slaves.

THE CARIBBEAN AFTER ABOLITION

Freed blacks in the Caribbean had to earn a living. The Emancipation Act of 1833 provided planters with £20 million in compensation for the loss of their free labour. However, ex-slaves themselves received nothing. For most black West Indians, the plantations were an unhappy reminder of their former lives, and they did not want to work there, even for wages. Some found employment by hiring themselves out as skilled labourers, for example as carpenters or cooks. Many more tried to set up small farms. However, the planters still needed labourers to work on their plantations. They made it difficult for black people to buy land, taxing its sale and refusing to break estates up into small, affordable farms. They evicted ex-slaves who would not work for them, or charged them absurdly high rents.

Some blacks overcame these obstacles. Many squatted illegally on unused plots of land. Others bought land direct from the British government, or clubbed together to buy a whole estate. Missionaries helped by buying large plantations, then dividing the land up and selling plots to black West Indians. In Jamaica, 40 per cent of land was owned by black people by 1860, while in Antigua land was so scarce that most ex-slaves were forced back to work on the plantations.

The Caribbean was hit by a crisis in its sugar industry when supporters of free trade in Britain (see page 48) finally got their way and taxes were abolished on foreign sugar. As a result, sugar from Cuba and Brazil became much cheaper than sugar from British colonies. More competition came from Europe, where a new method of producing cheap sugar from beet instead of cane had been developed. The planters were forced to reduce prices, which they achieved mainly by cutting their labourers' wages. Many planters went out of business, while others turned to more profitable crops such as coffee.

Despite these difficulties, the sugar industry began to recover in the 1850s. But there were severe labour shortages, particularly in Trinidad and British Guiana on the South American mainland. This problem was solved by the importation of indentured workers, known as coolies, from the Indian subcontinent. In total, about half a million Indians were brought to the Caribbean as part of the scheme, which ended in 1917.

Indian coolies at work on a cocoa plantation in Trinidad. These workers were treated little better than slaves.

THE MORANT BAY REBELLION

The sugar crisis hit Jamaica hard and black farmers were the most badly affected. One man, a Baptist deacon called Paul Bogle, decided the time had come to act. In 1865, Bogle tried to discuss the living conditions of the poor people on the island with the British governor. But Governor Eyre refused to see him. Two days later, hearing rumours of rebellion, Eyre sent the police to arrest Bogle. Bogle sent them back with the message that he would come to Morant Bay the next day. As promised, Bogle and several hundred supporters went to the courthouse in Morant Bay. Violence erupted, more than 20 people were killed and the courthouse was set on fire. The consequences for the black population were terrible. Soldiers killed more than 500 black people and burned down 1000 houses as they searched for Bogle. Bogle was eventually hanged.

The courthouse at Morant Bay, Jamaica, scene of the rebellion led by Paul Bogle in October 1865.

This extract is taken from the 'Ballad of Sixty Five' by Alma Norman. It describes the events of the Morant Bay Rebellion.

Stony Gut is the name of the area from where Paul Bogle and his supporters came.

The word **vestry** is used by the poet to describe the courthouse.

Kingston is the capital of Jamaica.

Stony Gut and Morant Bay are both in the parish of **St. Thomas**. Jamaica is divided into parishes in the same way as Britain is divided into counties.

The Monday morning was tropic clear
As the men from Stony Gut drew near,
Clenching their sticks in their farmer's hand
To claim their rights in their native land.

Oh many mourned and many were dead
That day when the vestry flames rose red.
There was chopping and shooting and when it
  done
Paul Bogle and his men knew they had to run.

They ran for the bush where they hoped to hide
But the soldiers poured in from Kingston side.
They took their prisoners to Morant Bay
Where they hanged them high in the early day.

Paul Bogle died but his spirit talks
Anywhere in Jamaica that freedom walks,
Where brave men gather and courage thrills
As it did in those days in St. Thomas hills.

THE ROAD TO WAR

Divisions between the North and South of the USA (see pages 36-7) grew worse as the 19th century progressed. The main argument concerned newly settled territories when they applied to become part of the USA. Should they allow slavery, like the Southern states, or forbid it, like those in the North? In 1820, Congress agreed to admit Missouri as a slave state and Maine as a free state. At the same time politicians voted for the Missouri Compromise, which drew an imaginary line across the USA. Slavery was to be legal in new states below this line, and illegal in new states above it.

This compromise worked for some years. However, problems arose over New Mexico, California and Utah, and later over the Kansas and Nebraska territories until, finally, the Kansas-Nebraska Act of 1854 abolished the Missouri Compromise. Eventually, disagreements between abolitionists in the North and supporters of slavery in the South led to the creation of the anti-slavery Republican Party.

During the 19th century, abolitionist activity flourished. In 1817, the American Colonization Society was formed by whites opposed to slavery. The Society established a colony in Liberia, West Africa, in 1821 and sent several thousand freed black people there. Soon, other voices were raised against slavery. In 1829, a free black man named David Walker wrote *An Appeal to the Colored Citizens of the World*, in which he called for the overthrow of slavery. In 1831, inspired by the emancipation campaign in Britain (see pages 48-9), white abolitionist William Lloyd Garrison launched a weekly anti-slavery journal called *The Liberator*. Many former slaves also campaigned long and hard for abolition in the USA. Among these abolitionists were black women such as Sojourner Truth and Maria Harper, and black men such as Charles Redmond and Frederick Douglass.

THE MISSOURI COMPROMISE AND AFTER

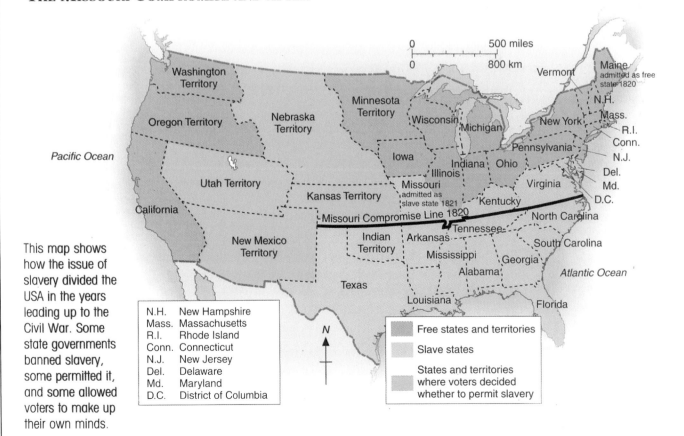

This map shows how the issue of slavery divided the USA in the years leading up to the Civil War. Some state governments banned slavery, some permitted it, and some allowed voters to make up their own minds.

N.H.   New Hampshire
Mass.   Massachusetts
R.I.   Rhode Island
Conn.   Connecticut
N.J.   New Jersey
Del.   Delaware
Md.   Maryland
D.C.   District of Columbia

Free states and territories

Slave states

States and territories where voters decided whether to permit slavery

Frederick Douglass publicised the message of abolition in Britain as well as in the USA, and gave many powerful speeches. He is also remembered for his autobiography, *Narrative of the Life of Frederick Douglass, an American Slave*, which was first published in 1845. This is an extract from it.

New Bedford is a port in Massachusetts.

The Liberator was William Lloyd Garrison's anti-slavery journal (see main text).

Douglass escaped from Maryland in 1838.

In about four months after I went to New Bedford, there came a young man to me, and inquired if I did not wish to take the Liberator. I told him I did; but just having made my escape from slavery, I remarked that I was unable to pay for it then. I, however, finally became a subscriber to it. The paper came, and I read it from week to week with such feelings as it would be quite idle for me to attempt to describe... Its sympathy for my brethren in bonds – its scathing denunciations of slaveholders – its faithful exposures of slavery – and its powerful attacks upon the upholders of the institution – sent a thrill of joy through my soul...

Sojourner Truth was born a slave in 1797, but escaped to freedom as an adult. She campaigned tirelessly for the anti-slavery cause in the USA, and later devoted herself to the struggle for women's rights.

Frederick Douglass

UNCLE TOM'S CABIN

A novel published in 1852 brought the horrors of slavery to a wider audience than ever before. This book was *Uncle Tom's Cabin* by Harriet Beecher Stowe. Stowe was born in the free state of Connecticut on the eastern coast of the USA. In 1832, she moved with her family to Ohio, which was next to the slave state of Kentucky. Here she witnessed slave-catchers kidnapping black runaways and forcing them back to the South. In 1850, Harriet set about writing a book to help the abolitionist cause. Her powerful story of ruthless slave-owner Simon Legree and kind-hearted slave Uncle Tom became an instant success.

135,000 SETS, 270,000 VOLUMES SOLD.

UNCLE TOM'S CABIN

FOR SALE HERE.

AN EDITION FOR THE MILLION, COMPLETE IN 1 Vol, PRICE 37 1-2 CENTS.
"   "   IN GERMAN, IN 1 Vol, PRICE 50 CENTS.
"   "   IN 2 Vols, CLOTH, 6 PLATES, PRICE $1.50.
SUPERB ILLUSTRATED EDITION, IN 1 Vol, WITH 153 ENGRAVINGS,
PRICES FROM $2.50 TO $5.00.

The Greatest Book of the Age.

THE AMERICAN CIVIL WAR

In autumn 1860, the first Republican president of the USA, Abraham Lincoln, was elected. The Southern states would not accept his leadership, and seven of them broke away from the United States. On 4 February 1861, representatives of these seven states established the Confederate States of America, known as the Confederacy, under Jefferson Davis. In April of the same year, the American Civil War began when Confederate soldiers attacked Fort Sumter in South Carolina. In May, four more slave states joined the Confederacy (see map).

Discipline on Southern plantations broke down during the Civil War exactly as it had done during the War of Independence (see pages 34-5). In their masters' absence, thousands of slaves began to disobey orders and 'go slow'. Thousands more, perhaps as many as half a million, left the plantations altogether and headed for the Union (Northern states) army, offering to fight against the Confederate enemy. As the Union faced a shortage of fighting men, the president made a decision that was to alter the character of the war.

On 1 January 1863, Abraham Lincoln issued the Emancipation Proclamation. This stated that all slaves in the Confederate States were free from that day onwards, and that they could become members of the Union army. About 90,000 freed blacks from the Southern states fought alongside a similar number from the North. Of the 600,000 soldiers and sailors who died during the war, at least 38,000 were blacks.

In the autumn of 1864, Lincoln was elected to a second term as president. As part of his campaign, he had promised to introduce an amendment to the constitution that would make slavery illegal throughout the USA. On 31 January 1865, this 13th Amendment was passed amid great rejoicing. By March 1865, the Confederacy was on the verge of defeat. Jefferson Davis decided to allow slaves to fight in the Southern army for the first time, in a desperate bid to turn the tide. But it was too late. On 9 April 1865, the main Southern forces surrendered. Just five days later, Abraham Lincoln was killed by a Confederate supporter called John Wilkes Booth.

UNION AND CONFEDERATE STATES

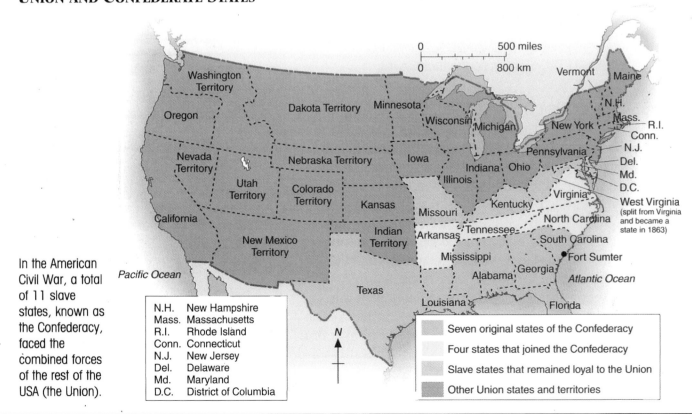

In the American Civil War, a total of 11 slave states, known as the Confederacy, faced the combined forces of the rest of the USA (the Union).

N.H.	New Hampshire
Mass.	Massachusetts
R.I.	Rhode Island
Conn.	Connecticut
N.J.	New Jersey
Del.	Delaware
Md.	Maryland
D.C.	District of Columbia

Seven original states of the Confederacy

Four states that joined the Confederacy

Slave states that remained loyal to the Union

Other Union states and territories

In the 1930s, researchers in the USA interviewed many former slaves as part of the Federal Writers' Project. By this time, most blacks who had been adults during the slavery era had died, but many who were children had vivid memories to record. One of these was Susie Melton, who remembered hearing the news of Lincoln's Emancipation Proclamation in 1863.

Niggers is an offensive word today, but it was the actual word used by Susie Melton (see page 6).

Missus means 'mistress', probably the wife of a plantation owner who was away fighting with the Confederate army.

Northern soldiers were known as **Yankees**.

Williamsburg is in Virginia.

'Mancipation' is short for Emancipation Proclamation.

I was a young gal, about ten years old, and we done heard that Lincoln gonna turn the **niggers** free. Ol' **missus** say there wasn't nothin' to it. Then a **Yankee** soldier told someone in **Williamsburg** that Lincoln done signed the **'mancipation**. Was wintertime and mighty cold that night, but everybody commenced getting ready to leave. Didn't care nothin' about missus – was going to the Union lines. And all that night the niggers danced and sang right out in the cold. Next morning at day break we all started out with blankets and clothes and pots and pans and chickens piled on our backs, 'cause missus said we couldn't take no horses or carts.

A SOLDIER'S PAY

Even in the Union army, black soldiers faced discrimination. They served in segregated black units under white officers and had to carry out the heaviest jobs, such as digging trenches. Despite this, black soldiers were paid $7 a month, compared to a white soldier's pay of $13. After many protests, Congress eventually made equal pay for blacks and whites in the army obligatory in June 1864.

Company E of the Union army's Fourth Colored Light Infantry, pictured in 1865.

RECONSTRUCTION

Once the Civil War was over, the USA was faced with several urgent tasks. The Confederate states had to be made part of the Union once more, and needed to be rebuilt following the devastation caused by the war. In addition, four million free black people had to establish their new roles in American society. The programme designed to accomplish all this was known as Reconstruction.

Following Lincoln's assassination, his Vice-President, Andrew Johnson, came to power. Johnson was a Southerner and was sympathetic to Southern concerns. He began Reconstruction in 1865 by setting up assemblies in all the former Confederate states. These assemblies had to approve the 13th Amendment, but were permitted to draw up constitutions that did not allow black people to vote. Many of the Southern states introduced Black Codes to restrict the rights of black people. Some Codes also allowed unemployed black people to be forced to work.

Congress tried to introduce measures to make the Black Codes illegal, but these were met with opposition from President Johnson. Nevertheless, in June 1866, the Republicans managed to pass the 14th Amendment to the Constitution. This granted citizenship to everyone born in the USA, and obliged states to give all Americans equal rights in law. Congress also voted to divide the Southern states into five military districts, and deny them self-rule until they adopted constitutions that accepted the 14th Amendment and gave blacks the vote. All the Southern states had such constitutions in place by 1870. In 1869 the 15th Amendment was passed. This made it an offence to deny a man the vote on the grounds of colour or race.

The framework was now in place for blacks, or at least black men, to play a role in American politics. Many served in state governments, while between 1868 and 1877, 16 black men were elected to the House of Representatives and two to the Senate. But their triumph was short-lived. States began to restrict the right to vote by introducing reading and writing tests, or insisting that voters owned property or had a certain amount of money. Congress ended the process of Reconstruction in 1877, when the last troops were withdrawn from the South.

The first seven black representatives to serve in the US Congress. The Congress is made up of two houses, the Senate and the House of Representatives.

Henry MacNeal Turner was a minister of the African Methodist Episcopal Church. In the Civil War he served as chaplain to soldiers in a black regiment of the Union army, and in 1867 was elected to the state government of Georgia. However, the government's white members voted to expel all blacks just one year later. This is an extract from a speech he made in protest at this event.

> Turner is speaking on behalf of all former slaves here.

> **Garner** means to 'gather'.

> **Curtailed** means 'shortened'.

Why, sir, though **we** are not white, we have accomplished much. We have pioneered civilization here; we have built up your country; we have worked in your fields, and **garnered** your harvests, for two hundred and fifty years! And what do we ask of you in return? Do we ask you for compensation for the sweat our fathers bore for you – for the tears you have caused, and the hearts you have broken, and the lives you have **curtailed**, and the blood you have spilled? Do we ask retaliation? We ask it not. We are willing to let the dead past bury its dead; but we ask you now for our RIGHTS...

THE FREEDMEN'S BUREAU

As part of Reconstruction, the American government set up the Freedmen's Bureau in 1865. The aim of the Bureau was to help both newly freed blacks and white planters to adjust to their new circumstances. It provided food for poor blacks and whites, helped free blacks to buy land and find employment, and paid for school- and hospital-building projects. Despite having few staff and a low budget, the Bureau did much excellent work. It was abolished in 1872.

For black people in the American South, living conditions, schooling and employment opportunities remained poor, even after the Civil War was over.

CONCLUSION

The hope felt by many blacks in the former slave colonies of the Americas after the abolition of slavery gradually faded. It gave way to the realisation that equality and fair treatment were still a distant dream.

In the Caribbean, conditions for the black inhabitants improved little. Most blacks farmed poor land and lived in inadequate housing. Few had access to decent education or medical services. Discrimination on racial grounds was widespread. Many people left the Caribbean in search of a better life. Some headed for Central America in the 1880s and early 1900s to help build the Panama Canal. Others went to Costa Rica and Honduras, where work was available on flourishing banana farms. Following the abolition of slavery in Cuba in 1886, thousands went there to look for work on the sugar plantations.

In the USA, the situation was equally bad. Once troops left the South in 1877, many aspects of the old way of life began to re-emerge. White politicians took control of state governments. The American government gave back huge farms to the white plantation owners, but did little to help blacks buy even small plots of land. As a result, many former slaves ended up working in the fields of rich white men, just as they had before the Civil War. At the same time, there was an increase in white violence against the newly freed blacks. Beatings, burnings and even lynchings (executions) were regularly carried out by neighbourhood groups and secret racist societies such as the Ku Klux Klan.

By the early 20th century, state governments throughout the USA had restricted blacks' rights and introduced segregation in almost every public place, from playgrounds to hospitals and schools. Throughout the Americas, emancipation had arrived, but equality was not even in sight.

The Ku Klux Klan was formed in Tennessee in 1865, and soon spread across the American South. The organisation still exists today.

A Florida bar for blacks only in 1945. Blacks and whites were segregated by law in the USA until the Civil Rights Acts were passed in the late 1950s and early 1960s.

In the 1960s, the great American activist Martin Luther King led the continuing fight for black civil rights. On 28 August 1963, a hundred years after Abraham Lincoln issued the Emancipation Proclamation, King led a march of 210,000 black Americans to the Lincoln Memorial in Washington D.C. The case for the rights of blacks in the Americas has never been better or more movingly expressed than it was in his speech on that day. This is part of that speech:

The **great American** to whom King is referring is Abraham Lincoln.

A **score** equals 20, so five score is 100.

This is a quotation from the Declaration of Independence (see page 35).

Martin Luther King preached non-violent resistance to the authorities. Tragically, in 1968 he was assassinated in Memphis, Tennessee.

Five score years ago, a great American, in whose symbolic shadow we stand, signed the Emancipation Proclamation. This momentous decree came as a great beacon light of hope to millions of Negro slaves who had been seared in the flame of withering injustice. It came as a joyous daybreak to end the long night of captivity... But one hundred years later, we must face the fact that the Negro is still not free... I have a dream that one day this nation will rise up and live out the true meaning of its creed: 'We hold these truths to be self-evident; that all men are created equal.' I have a dream that one day on the red hills of Georgia the sons of former slaves and the sons of former slaveowners will be able to sit down together at the table of brotherhood... I have a dream today.

GLOSSARY

abolition the act of bringing something to an end, or abolishing it. People who campaigned for the abolition of slavery were known as abolitionists.

apprenticeship the changeover period following the abolition of slavery in the British colonies in 1833. During this time, most slaves were not fully free and had to continue working for their masters. Apprenticeship came to an end in 1838.

auction a type of slave sale during which buyers made bids for the slaves they wanted to purchase. Auctions are run by auctioneers.

Baptist a member of a Protestant Christian group founded in the 17th century. The group teaches that only believers who are old enough to understand and accept Christianity for themselves should be baptised.

barracoon a dungeon or pen, often underground, in a European trading fort. Captured Africans were kept in barracoons until the slavers were ready to load them on to ships.

bayonet a blade attached to the top of a gun.

billhook a large knife with a wooden handle and a curved blade used for cutting sugar cane.

brand to burn an owner's mark into the skin with a piece of heated iron or other metal.

caravan a group of traders travelling through the desert, usually accompanied by camels carrying their goods.

Caribbean Sea a sea that forms part of the Atlantic Ocean. It is bordered by the Caribbean Islands to the north and east, Central America to the west, and South America to the south.

colony a country governed by the rulers of another state.

compensation money or goods given to make up for damage or loss.

Confederacy the 11 states of the American South that broke away from the USA in 1861 and sparked off the American Civil War (1861-5).

Congress the law-making body of the USA, which consists of two houses, the Senate and the House of Representatives.

conquistador a Spanish word meaning 'conqueror'. It is used to describe all the Spanish invaders who colonised lands in the Americas during the 16th century.

constitution the basic political principles according to which a nation is governed. The constitution of the USA is a written constitution, which came into effect in 1789.

coolie an indentured labourer brought to some British colonies from India following the abolition of slavery.

discrimination ill-treatment on the grounds of race or other characteristic such as class or religion.

dysentery an intestinal infection that causes severe diarrhoea.

emancipation the act of freeing, or being freed.

free trade trade without government interference, for example in the form of taxes.

gang system a system of slave labour in which field slaves were divided into different gangs according to their age and fitness. The 'great gang' or 'first gang' carried out the most punishing work, while the 'small gang' or 'second gang' did lighter work such as weeding.

Hispaniola an island in the Caribbean discovered by Christopher Columbus in 1492. He claimed it for the Spanish and called it La Isla Española (the Spanish island). In 1697, the western section of the island was granted to the French. It became known as St Domingue, while the eastern, Spanish section was called Santo Domingo. Today, Hispaniola is divided into Haiti in the west and the Dominican Republic in the east.

indenture a formal contract between servant and master. An indentured servant is tied to his or her master by such a contract.

Industrial Revolution the period in the 18th and 19th centuries during which Britain changed

from being an agricultural society, where most people worked on the land, to an industrial society, where most people worked in factories. The same process took place in the rest of Western Europe and the USA shortly afterwards.

manumission the freeing of a slave by his or her owner. Some slaves were granted freedom others saved to buy it.

Maroon a runaway slave living in a community of other fugitives in the Caribbean or on the American mainland. Descendants of runaways who lived in the same communities were also known as Maroons.

Methodist a member of a Protestant Christian group founded in the 18th century by Charles and John Wesley. At first Methodists formed a section within the Church of England, but in the 1790s broke away to form their own organisation.

missionary a person who preaches his or her religion to other people in order to convert them. Many missionaries also carry out charitable work, such as feeding and housing the poor.

molasses a type of dark syrup obtained from sugar cane during the refining process.

obeah a type of religion practised by slaves in some parts of the Caribbean. Obeah priests tried to influence the world of the spirits by carrying out special rituals.

Patriot army the army of the American rebels during the American War of Independence (1775-83).

plantation a large estate where crops such as sugar or cotton are grown.

planter a plantation owner.

Presbyterian a member of a Protestant Christian group founded in the 16th century. Presbyterian churches are governed by elders.

Quaker a member of a Christian group founder in the 17th century by George Fox. Quakers worship simply, without priests or rituals, and have been involved in many campaigns for social justice.

Reconstruction the 12-year period (1865-77) following the American Civil War during which the Confederacy was rebuilt and made part of the USA once more.

Sabbath Sunday, the day that Christians believe should be used for worship and rest.

scramble a type of slave sale during which slaves were enclosed in a confined area such as a room or yard. Buyers then rushed in at an appointed time and grabbed anyone they wished to purchase.

seasoning the process of introducing new slaves to plantation work by giving them relatively simple tasks to do, such as weeding.

segregation separation or isolation, for example on the grounds of race or colour.

shackles metal rings fastened around the wrists or ankles of a prisoner to limit movement.

slave-driver a man employed by a slave-owner to supervise slaves and to punish slacking or poor work.

smallpox a serious and extremely contagious disease. It causes high fever and a severe rash that leaves deep scars.

Sudan the region of Africa between the Sahara to the north and the tropics to the south. (Sudan is also the name of a modern country in northeast Africa.)

task system a system of slave labour in which field slaves were given a particular task to complete in a day. Only when the task was finished were slaves allowed to return to their cabins or tend their own gardens.

Underground Railroad a network of road and sea routes along which slaves escaped from the slave states of the American South to the free states of the North. Some sections of the railroad continued over the northern border of the USA into Canada.

Union the states that remained in the USA during the American Civil War (1861-5) and fought the Confederacy.

INDEX